VEGETARIAN MEALS

for People-on-the-Go

VEGGIE WRAP COMBINATIONS, SEE PAGE 80

VEGETARIAN MEALS

for People-on-the-Go

101 QUICK & EASY RECIPES

Vimala Rodgers

Hay House, Inc.
Carlsbad, California • Sydney, Australia
Canada • Hong Kong • United Kingdom

Copyright © 2002 by Vimala Rodgers

Published and distributed in the United States by:
  Hay House, Inc., P.O. Box 5100, Carlsbad, CA 92018-5100
  (800) 654-5126 • (800) 650-5115 (fax) • www.hayhouse.com /
  Hay House Australia Pty Ltd, P.O. Box 515, Brighton-Le-Sands NSW 2216
  1800 023 516 • *e-mail:* info@hayhouse.com.au

EDITORIAL SUPERVISION: Jill Kramer
PRODUCED FOR HAY HOUSE BY LANSDOWNE PUBLISHING, AUSTRALIA
PROJECT COORDINATOR: Bettina Hodgson
DESIGNER: Avril Makula
PHOTOGRAPHER: Amanda McLauchlan
STYLIST: Michaela le Compte
FOOD STYLIST'S ASSISTANTS: Rodney Dunn, Steve Pearce
FOOD: With thanks to Antico's Fruitworld, Northbridge
PROPS: Papaya Studios, Empire Homewares, Funkis Swedish Form, Made in Japan, Major & Tom,
Planet Furniture, Bisanna Tiles, Cloth, Ruby Star Traders, Domestic Pots, Carmague, The Baytree
PHOTOGRAPHY PP 23, 30, 35, 38, 83, 138, 158, 171: Maree Homer, STYLED BY: Vicki Liley

Library of Congress Cataloging-in-Publication Data

Rodgers, Vimala.
  Vegetarian meals for people-on-the-go : 101 quick & easy recipes / Vimala Rodgers.
     p. cm.
  Includes index.
  ISBN 1-56170-843-7 (hardcover)
  1. Vegetarian cookery. 2. Quick and easy cookery. I. Title.

TX837 .R737 2002
641.5'636—dc21

                                                            2001051468

                              ISBN 1-56170-843-7

                         05 04 03 02   4 3 2 1
                          1st printing, May 2002

                          Printed in Singapore

I dedicate this book to John Robbins

Contents

Gravies, Sauces & Condiments • 115

Brown Baggin' It • 123

Go Lightly: Breakfast • 131

SIOBHAN'S GREEK BEANS, SEE PAGE 85

Acknowledgments

Deepest appreciation to my dear friend Sister Catherine Connell, who, in earlier years, gave me permission to be fully alive. Then, in 1989, it was she who dragged me to a health-food store and insisted that I purchase John Robbins' book, *Diet for a New America*. The rest is history.

Much gratitude to Louise Hay for her many kindnesses and her unfailing support, and to 'Hay Housers' Jill Kramer and Christy Salinas for their awesome, upbeat attitudes and their enlightened openness. Such gifts!

This book would still be whirling about randomly in my head, had not a friend said, "I'll typeset it for you." An expert in her field, she volunteered hundreds of hours to giving this book its first real form, a gift I shall never forget. Assembling a cookbook is a massive undertaking, and for doing it with such a light heart, I gratefully acknowledge Maggie Shank, without whom you would not be holding this book in your hands.

And of course . . .
A "Fourth of July Rockets Red Glare" **thank you** to all my incredible children, each so gorgeously different from the other, in whom courage, brilliance, and a relentless sense of humor have always flourished wildly! These qualities were called upon again and again as I bumbled my way through the process of learning how to be a mom—and how to cook naturally, often guessing my way through it all. Although my children are adults now, their distinguishing traits have not changed. Jean-Marie, Stephanie, Siobhan, Matthew-John, Mark, Amanda, Sara, and Luke—I offer you my sincerest appreciation, love, and greatest respect. What an outrageous adventure!

"Nothing will benefit human health and increase the chances for survival on earth as much as the evolution of a vegetarian diet."
— ALBERT EINSTEIN

INTRODUCTION:
ABOUT THE BOOK

*"Let your medicines be your food
and your foods be your medicine."*
— HIPPOCRATES

Introduction: About the Book

I became a vegetarian in 1969. Because it was virtually an unknown lifestyle at the time, I had no magazines, recipes, or health-food stores to depend on for menus and information. Although nutrition education became a necessary component of my new diet, it took me at least five years before I felt I had really caught on to preparing balanced and tasty meals. Fortunately for my family and me, our doctor was a Seventh-Day Adventist, the only person I knew who had an extensive educational background in nutrition. While he knew very little about meal preparation, Dr. Lloyd Pratt became my guardian angel when it came to learning about minerals, enzymes, amino acids, vitamins, and the thousands of other components the body requires for sound, trouble-free functioning.

I mention this so you'll know that the recipes in this book are based not only on ease of preparation and taste, but on sound nutritional principles as well. Although some recipes worked the first time around, most are the product of much experimentation, many redoes, and countless shuffling of ingredients to suit the fussiest palate—from high chair through high school age and well beyond. I learned the hard way—through trial and error. Ask my children: I had eight of them. They were my primary taste-testers.

I've written this book for the many people who are beginning to question their eating habits and relate them to the state of their health. Although newsstands are filled with information on diet and health, how to eat better, vegetarianism, and the like, many of those whom I know and love don't have a clue where to start, and they simply don't have spare time to spend in the kitchen.

This book is a basic answer to the question: "I'd love to stop eating meat, but what do I eat instead?" Up until now, my response has been to share recipes, menus, and nutritional tips—most of which have remained in my head or on 3 x 5 cards in my old wooden recipe box. But since an astounding number of people have continued to ask that question, I decided to put this book together.

This work has one purpose: to make the transition to a vegetarian diet natural, effortless, quick, and a whole lot of fun. Some of the recipes are my own, some came from my daughters, and others came from places long forgotten. Credit has been given appropriately.

The recipes have been chosen carefully for delectability, general appeal, and ease of preparation; more than half of them can be prepared by children as young as eight years old. Even though I enjoy cooking, I like to be in and out of the kitchen as quickly as possible. These recipes allow me to do that, with most of the preparation time being less than 30 minutes.

All of the recipes have been tested and retested by friends who have requested them, my houseguests, patrons in the fine restaurants in which my daughters have worked as chefs, and the most rigorous testers known to any cook: my children as they were growing up.

We were not a quiet, low-key family; my children were and still are vigorous, healthy, caring, independent, self-determined, and beautiful. They never let me get away with anything at mealtime. If you have children, you know what I mean.

I remember the first time I casually sprinkled mung bean sprouts over the green salad. My then-ten-year-old son, Mark, looked at it thoughtfully, glanced around the table at his brothers and sisters, and said, "Hey, Mom, I thought you were a vegetarian." His brief pause was dramatic. He looked up and continued, "So why did you put slug eggs all over the lettuce?" Ah, those were the days.

I've designed each recipe so that it can be tailored to suit your taste, or your family's taste. No recipes are carved in stone; each one is open to your versatile touch. The word you will see (or which will be implied) again and again in these pages is *experiment!* Consider it an invitation to use your creative personal touch. If you're out of a vegetable or grain that the recipe calls for, use the one you have. If you're out of a particular seasoning or herb, try another.

As far as the setup of the book is concerned, over the years, I've discovered many shortcuts to vegetarian cooking. I've included them in the **Tips & Shortcuts** section at the beginning of almost every chapter and part. I invite you to keep a log of your own.

A FEW HEALTH BENEFITS & STATISTICS

In 1996, the U.S. Surgeon General reported that 68 percent of all deaths in this country resulted from diet-related disease. Diets high in saturated fat and cholesterol—substances found primarily or exclusively in meat, poultry, and dairy products—play a major causative role in maladies such as heart disease, strokes, kidney disease, osteoporosis, and many types of cancer.

Healthy Heart
You reduce your risk of heart attack by 90 percent on a pure vegetarian diet, by 45 percent if you reduce your present consumption of meat, dairy products, and eggs by half.

Cancer
World populations with a high meat intake have high rates of colon cancer; those with a low meat intake have correspondingly low rates. The risk of breast cancer is four times higher for women who eat meat daily compared to women who eat meat less than once a week. Women who eat eggs daily compared to those

who eat eggs less than once a week have a three-times-higher rate of contracting breast cancer.

Cholesterol

You have more than a 50 percent chance of dying from a disease caused by clogged arteries if your blood cholesterol is "normal"; this risk is reduced to 5 percent if you don't consume saturated fat. The leading sources of saturated fat and cholesterol in American diets are meat, dairy products, and eggs. The only dietary source of cholesterol is an animal product; our liver manufactures all we need.

Osteoporosis

Osteoporosis and kidney failure are two diseases that are directly linked to excess protein consumption. There are tens of millions of cases of osteoporosis and kidney failure in the United States. The average measurable bone loss of female meat-eaters at age 65 is 35 percent. The average measurable bone loss of female vegetarians at age 65 is 18 percent.

All recipes in this book eliminate meat, fish, chicken, eggs, and dairy products, with one exception: ghee. Ghee is butter with the milk solids removed; it is also called clarified butter. To find out the history of ghee, why I recommend it, and how to make your own, turn to Chapter 2, "Main Dishes."

Most of us know how carrots, lettuce, kale, potatoes, and spinach grow, since many of us have planted, tended, and harvested our own gardens. Some of us have seen, walked through, or picked fruit in an orchard. There's nothing to compare with the experience of picking a piece of ripe fruit and biting into it while standing beneath the tree of its origin. It's almost a sacred feeling.

The process of raising animals as food for the table, however, is kept a closely guarded secret by the meat industry. You'll never see a third-grade class on a field trip to a factory farm or slaughterhouse, nor will they ever be featured on *Sesame Street* or the Discovery Channel.

Do you want to choose more consciously about the food that goes into your body? Are you even a little bit curious about the origin of that steak, veal chop, hamburger, or plate of Chicken McNuggets you had last week? If so, an excellent source of accurate information is the book *Diet for a New America*, by John Robbins. It has no recipes. It has no opinions. It contains only well-documented data on our food-eating habits. It will give you a boost as you begin to shop consciously for the sake of your health. Read it, then choose. How and what you decide is up to you.

The unfolding theme for the 21st century is *conscious choices*. Maintaining a pure vegetarian diet is a significant part of what that's all about. Eating consciously is taking a self-determined step toward being responsible for our choices and our health, and seeing how those choices impact every other living thing on the planet.

My approach does not have to be yours. As I began to discover what healthful eating was all about, in one fell swoop I cleared my kitchen of any food that might be considered detrimental to my family's health. Our cupboards were almost bare. "Don't panic; I have a plan," I told the kids. "We're going to be healthier than ever!" Was this an extreme solution? This story may help you decide.

When my oldest son, Matthew, became a seventh-grader, he enrolled in a Catholic school. I had known the principal for years and was thrilled at the change. His second day there, I received a call from her. Her opening words, "Are you sitting down?" caused a knee-jerk reaction. *"Is anything wrong, Louise? Is Matthew okay?!"* The principal continued, "Well"—she was stifling a chuckle—"yesterday all the new students had to fill in emergency forms. On one line it asked for 'religion.' Matthew wrote: 'vegetarian.' I called him into my office just now and told him that vegetarianism was not a religion. Without so much as blinking, he replied, 'You don't know my mother very well.'"

∾

AUTHOR'S NOTE: Within some recipes, and in portions of the text, the names of certain dishes are printed in bold to signify that they have their own listing elsewhere in the book (e.g., **Ghee** or **Basic Marinara Sauce**).

BELL PEPPER EXTRAVAGANZA, SEE PAGE 84

BEFORE YOU BEGIN

"The unfolding theme for the 21st century is conscious choices.
Maintaining a pure vegetarian diet is a significant part
of what that's all about."

— VIMALA

The Basics of Vegetarian Cooking

EATING TIPS & SHORTCUTS

❖ Buy organic whenever possible—be kind to your body. Conventional growers use chemical fertilizers, soil fumigants, and pesticides. Distributors and food markets use dyes and wax, and they sometimes dip and spray vegetables to retard spoilage. With the advent of biogenetic engineering—and the government's decision that genetically restructured fruits and vegetables need not be labeled thus—it's impossible to know whether any fruit or vegetable you buy has been chemically altered through the use of pig—or other animal or fish—genes. Under current regulations, organic food cannot be genetically modified. You can ask your greengrocers about the treatment of the produce they carry, yet they may not have been informed.

❖ Ask your grocers to order organic produce. If they don't know where they can obtain it, go to the library or the Internet and find out, then share the information with them. If they balk, go to another grocer.

❖ If organic produce is not available, or if it's available but very expensive, buy regular vegetables and wash them again and again with undiluted apple cider vinegar. Don't just casually rinse them before you prepare them.

❖ Nutritionally, nuts, bananas, and avocados are excellent meat substitutes.

❖ Raw green salads are best eaten before a meal, as the enzymes they contain aid digestion.

❖ Include as much raw food in your diet as possible. Raw food and other fibrous foods act as brooms to sweep the intestines clean. They also improve calcium metabolism and strengthen heart and nerve tissue.

❖ Drink water 30 minutes before or after meals but not with them; fluids dilute digestive juices and hamper digestion.

❖ Your body welcomes foods that are alkaline. It feels attacked by those that are acid-forming, such as coffee, alcohol, flesh foods, and dairy products.

❖ Use nut spreads as a filler to replace eggs in casseroles, natural burgers, and grain or nut loaves. Organic peanut butter, tahini (from hulled sesame seeds), or almond butter are all excellent alternatives.

❖ Don't cook or bake in aluminum pots/pans, and *read labels carefully for aluminum* as a subtle ingredient. Since 1885, aluminum has been known to be toxic to nervous tissues. It's a poison that can be either ingested, absorbed through the skin, or inhaled. Read your labels! Cake mixes, baking soda, baking powder, instant chocolate mixes (which contain aluminum maltol), deodorants, skin lotions, facial creams, quick-loss diet tablets, and mouth sprays are the obvious culprits to be avoided. (John A. McDougall, *The McDougall Program: Twelve Days to Dynamic Health*.)

❖ Use baking soda only for putting out kitchen fires or drawing out the toxins from a bee sting (vinegar for a wasp sting). Soda destroys some of the vitamin content of food, especially the precious B complex vitamins.

❖ Avoid using cornstarch unless powdering a baby's bottom, as it inhibits digestion. Instead, use arrowroot powder as a thickener.

❖ Watch your protein intake. The importance of protein has been highly overrated. Contrary to what we were told growing up, it is not the angel of good health we were led to believe. An excess of protein is, in fact, the main cause of osteoporosis, that disease which is a result of gradual bone mineral losses. It causes more deaths in women than cancer of the breast and cervix combined.

"Osteoporosis is, in fact, a disease caused by a number of things, the most important of which is excess dietary protein." (Johnson, N., et al, "Effect of Level of Protein Intake on Urinary and Fecal Calcium and Calcium Retention," *Journal of Nutrition*, 100: 1425. 1970.)

Dr. John McDougall summarized it clearly when he stated, ". . . the most important dietary change that we can make if we want to create a positive calcium balance that will keep our bones solid is to decrease the amount of protein we eat each day. The important change is not to increase the amount of calcium we take in."

FOOD COMBINING

Quite a bit has been written about food combining, so rather than go into a lot of detail, here is a list that should make it easy.

These Combinations Are Friendly
❖ Vegetables: with grains, pasta, tofu, beans
❖ Fruit: alone when raw; when cooked, with grains or nuts
❖ Melon: always with nothing else; and watermelon with no other melon, just watermelon

These Combinations Are Gas-Forming
❖ Fruit: with beans, vegetables, dairy products, or meat

❖ Grain: with dairy products or meat

❖ Melons: with anything else

Those who eat according to a macrobiotic diet always say to eat fruit cooked. I have friends who have been critically ill and have healed their bodies by maintaining a strict macrobiotic diet.

I know other people who always say to eat fruit raw, and, like my macrobiotic friends, have healed their bodies. The one factor omitted by those who say we all must eat a certain way to attain optimum health is that we do not all have the same body types.

These days, there is an abundance of information available on body types and diet. I've included a selection of valuable resources at the end of the book. Experiment with various recipes to see how your body feels. I don't know of a better guideline.

Natural Laxatives
❖ Prunes
❖ Watermelon
❖ Melons
❖ Tomatoes
❖ Figs
❖ Raisins
❖ Grapes

CLEANING UP YOUR ACT

If you want to gain maximum health benefits from a diet that is as toxin-free and natural as possible, it's helpful to rid the body of toxins that already reside there. This is especially important if you have problems with elimination. When the body becomes constipated, toxins have a field day and can cause all kinds of damage. If you've been a red-meat eater most of your life, it might be a good idea to consider the following system of eating for a few days. It has the ability to cleanse the entire intestinal tract. The longer you're on it, the better cleaning job it can do.

Of all the cleansing diets out there, I've found this one to be the easiest to follow and also the most thorough. Besides, you're never hungry; and it's all good, basic food. Simply stated, it's easy and it works. Following it for three to five days will work wonders.

CLEANSING DIET

Each day eat only these foods, and all of these foods.
Do not make any substitutions.

2 grapefruits
1 raw vegetable salad
5 oranges
1 cooked vegetable
2 lemons or limes (you can squirt them over the salad)
One quart **High-Energy Potassium Drink** (recipe follows)

HIGH-ENERGY POTASSIUM DRINK
5 cups water
1 bunch raw spinach
2 ribs raw celery
1 bunch raw parsley
5 raw carrots
No salt or spices of any kind

Scrub and chop all vegetables well. A food processor is ideal here. Place carrots and celery in boiling water, and boil for 10 minutes, keeping at a low boil. Add chopped spinach and parsley, and cook another 10 minutes. When the cooking time is up, put a colander over a 2-quart bowl, and pour the vegetable mixture into it. Let it drain well. You can squish it down to hasten the process if you want to. Drink the beverage throughout the day, warm or cold. It's extremely beneficial in alleviating indigestion and reducing the physical effects of stress. It also reduces chronic pain in the lower back and joints, especially when associated with rheumatism and arthritis. It will keep your energy high and dramatically reduce any craving for junk foods.

When you're on the Cleansing Diet and finish the Energy Drink before the end of the day, feel free to drink as much water as you'd like if you get thirsty.

If you feel the need for a pick-me-up during the day, use a blender to grind 10 raw almonds until they're a fine powder, then spin with one cup orange juice.

Follow this diet faithfully for a few days and your body will thank you again and again.

This cleansing program is high in electrolytes and is an exceedingly rich source of potassium. If it has been recommended that you limit the above foods in your diet for some reason, you might want to run this cleansing program by your health practitioner before you use it.

STOCKING YOUR CUPBOARD

The most valuable asset to have on hand as you begin to reshape your diet is a kitchen stocked with items that, once in your cupboard, will allow you to prepare a spectacular meal with ease. As you start using the recipes, you will learn hands-on how they can be used. Select what works for you, and experiment now and again with something you've never tried. It's the surest way to discover new favorites.

When I first began to cook vegetarian meals, I often heard the word *substitute*. I found out very quickly that for some food items there are no substitutes. Chocolate is not carob. Coffee is not herb tea. Meat is not tofu. So please know that I'm not suggesting for one moment that you substitute anything for the taste of meat products. I *am* suggesting that you use foods in place of them that *don't* taste like them. You may find that they taste even better than the "real" thing.

If you're concerned about the complete health of your body, I suggest that you do one thing when you go shopping for any food product: *Read the ingredients on the label.* The information that's hidden in hard-to-read three-point type may startle you.

On to the Simple Basics. Let's begin with seasonings.

SEASONINGS

Tamari

If you're reducing your salt intake, have a sensitivity to wheat, or want to avoid foods with preservatives, you may want to use tamari or tamari light instead of soy sauce. Regular soy sauce contains wheat with either alcohol or sodium benzoate added as a preservative. Shoyu also uses wheat as a filler. If you want pure soy sauce that is wheat-free and preservative-free, use tamari. Check the label carefully, as there are bottles boldly labeled *tamari* that are actually regular soy sauce. Check the ingredients to see if wheat or preservatives are present.

Throughout this book, I mention the brand names of several products. The reason I do so is that with greening and vegetarianism becoming such a profitable marketing focus, there are now countless products on the market that may sound nutritious but are actually loaded with junk. I mention the names of easy-to-obtain products that I know to be pure—and have had success with.

Dr. Bronner's Balanced-Mineral-Bouillon

This is a basic ingredient you can create instant stock for soups or gravies from. Any product with the *Dr. Bronner's* imprimatur is pristine pure: no hidden ingredients, no preservatives or chemicals. This includes baked corn or cheese snacks (as opposed to deep fried), and even Castile soap in lavender, rose, eucalyptus, almond, lemon, or peppermint scents.

I began using Dr. Bronner's products in the early '70s because they were trusted for their purity and integrity. I still use them. Each product carries its own sermonette, which adds that charming final touch.

Vegetable Bouillon Cubes or Paste

Read the tiny print on the label, as many bouillon cubes or bouillon pastes contain monosodium glutamate (MSG). Bouillon is great for making a quick soup or gravy stock. It's a tad saltier than Dr. Bronner's, with a little more vegetable flavor.

Whole Sea Salt

Whole sea salt differs from regular commercial table salt in that it comes from seawater that has been vacuum-dried at low temperatures and, as such, retains all the seawater minerals. This is not true of commercial table salt. Whole sea salt is not white, despite some of the "sea salt" found in health-food stores. Whole natural sea salt is slightly gray and occurs in larger crystals, granules, or powder. Brands currently available are *Muramoto* and *Sí* from Mexico, and *Maldon* from England.

Spike®

This all-purpose seasoning is well known by any long-time vegetarian. An unbelievable assortment of combined herbs lends spectacular flavor to any food you sprinkle this on or in. It's a must on avocados. I've found no other seasoning to compare with *Spike®*. Just reading the ingredients can make your mouth water.

Nutritional Yeast

Don't confuse this with Brewer's yeast, which has a completely different texture, flavor, and chemical composition. Not a seasoning per se, but rather a flavor and nutrition enhancer, nutritional yeast is a *sine qua non* for the vegetarian diet because it's an excellent source of vitamin B12. It adds a tantalizingly nutty flavor to soups, dips, and casseroles. I like to sprinkle it over my green salads before I toss them. I prefer using the wide-flake variety because the powdered form is so fine that it makes everyone sneeze! Mix one tablespoon in your dog's daily food so that he or she won't get fleas.

These are seasonings that can make or break a recipe. They're subtle. Delicate. Sometimes zingy. They make a difference that people will comment on. Experiment with combinations.

CONDIMENTS

Apple Cider Vinegar

Exceedingly high in potassium and a natural healer of many ailments—especially digestive and circulatory ones—this is actually the only vinegar that our human digestive tract finds agreeable. It contains malic acid, an ingredient necessary for proper digestion, whereas all other vinegars contain acetic acid, which actually interferes with the digestive processes.

Hippocrates (400 B.C.), known as the "father of medicine," frequently spoke of the healing properties of apple cider vinegar, and recommended it for its cleansing, healing, and energizing properties.

According to Henry G. Bieler, M.D., "The most harmful effect of [non-apple cider] vinegar in the body is that it tends to leech out the body's phosphorous and also stimulate the thyroid gland. As the phosphorous becomes depleted, the adrenal function diminishes, since phosphorous is one of the active components of adrenal secretion." (Henry G. Bieler, M. D., *Food is Your Best Medicine.*)

Above all, buy organic, but if you can't, this inexpensive liquid is also wonderful for rinsing your vegetables before you prepare them, as it dissolves surface preservatives and chemicals. I keep an attractive jar on the window ledge above my sink labeled "veggie wash." Contents? Apple cider vinegar. *Only* apple cider vinegar.

I've used *Bragg* apple cider vinegar exclusively for over 30 years; its quality and purity cannot be topped.

It is raw, unfiltered, organic, aged in wood, and the company has been producing pure, health-oriented foods for well over 80 years. For more information, go to: **www.bragg.com**.

Eggless Mayonnaise

It takes about seven minutes to make your own eggless mayonnaise (see **Tofu Mayonnaise,** pg.122). For your health's sake, avoid mayonnaise or any oil-based product made from either cottonseed or canola oils. Tops for both taste and health, my favorite commercial mayonnaise is *Vegenaise®*, manufactured by "Follow Your Heart." They also offer a mayonnaise made with canola oil—a big "no-no" for the conscious eater. As this book was going to press, their grapeseed mayo had a purple label. Read the label carefully to be sure what you're buying.

Mustards

For a splendidly subtle gourmet touch to any sandwich, use a stone-ground mustard that has no artificial anything. *Maille* has a fantastic Dijon green herb mustard with flavors that will keep you guessing as to the herbs it contains. Try it once, and it may become a standard in your condiment lineup.

Tahini

This spread, made from hulled sesame seeds, has an unusually pleasant taste and is excellent in nut or grain loaves as a filler instead of eggs. Extremely versatile, tahini is zingy as a sandwich spread and mysterious as the key ingredient in a salad dressing. Sesame butter is a spread made from sesame seeds with their hulls left on. These hulls contain a substantial amount of oxalic acid, which blocks absorption of calcium and other minerals. Oxalic acid is also what kidney stones are made of. For the above reasons, I use tahini exclusively.

Hoisin Sauce

Available in the Asian foods section of your supermarket, hoisin sauce is the ideal quick and easy sauce for virtually any stir-fry dishes made with tofu and green leafy vegetables.

Monosodium Glutamate (MSG)

To be avoided.

"MSG has many names. As it is becoming more widely known to be detrimental to health, the processed food industry, which uses it widely, is disguising it with such impressive names as hydrolyzed vegetable protein, hydrolyzed protein, plant protein extract, sodium caseinate, calcium caseinate, yeast extract, textured protein, autolyzed yeast, hydrolyzed oat flour." (Joyce Craddick, M.D., *Hidden Sources of MSG*, 1996.)

MSG is a flavor enhancer often used in Asian cooking, and instant cups of soup and canned soups as well. "The safest rule is not to buy it. . . . What it does is to irritate the wall of the stomach to a stage of bright red acute congestion. The acute congestion causes hunger sensations so you ask for a second helping. . . . When the public realizes that acute congestion of the stomach is an almost ideal way to induce cancer in that organ in susceptible individuals, canned soups will change their ways." Those are the words of Blake F. Donaldson, M.D., in his book *Strong Medicine*. MSG is also known to cause severe migraine headaches.

HERBS

For those occasions when you want to add the sensuous touch that transforms the ordinary meal into a gourmet delight, use one or a combination of the following herbs. Half-pint canning jars work well for dried herb storage, are inexpensive, attractive, and can be used again and again for a multitude of purposes. If you are fortunate enough to have fresh herbs available to you, use them as your first choice over dried.

Although I am listing a few basics to choose from, experiment with new discoveries. If herbs are new to you, follow the guidelines at first. Once you feel comfortable, mix and match. Create your own special flavor and accent. It's all a matter of taste—yours! List the ways you like them best.

Herb Enhancers

Possible Uses	**"My Favorite Uses"**

ANISE
- Applesauce
- Baked apples

OREGANO
- Tomato-based dishes
- Fresh, in salads

DILL
- Potato salad
- Legume soups
- Gravies
- Sauerkraut

GARLIC
- Soups & stews
- Sauces
- Vegetables
- Bread spread
- Potatoes
- Almost any salad or vegetable

Herb Enhancers

Possible Uses   **"My Favorite Uses"**

GINGER (FRESH WHEN POSSIBLE)

- Soups & stews
- Sauces
- Teas
- Asian dishes
- East Indian dishes

PAPRIKA

- Garnish for salads
- Vegetables, especially potatoes
- Seasoning in homemade mayonnaise

PARSLEY (FRESH WHEN POSSIBLE)

- Soups & stews
- Salads
- Casseroles
- Beverages, when juiced with other vegetables
- Tofu dishes
- Most vegetables

MARJORAM

- Tomato-based dishes
- Salads
- Soups & stews

Herb Enhancers

Possible Uses   **"My Favorite Uses"**

MINT

- Peppermint, spearmint
- Dressings & sauces
- Teas, hot & iced
- Fruit salads
- Applesauce
- In smoothies

NASTURTIUM LEAVES & FLOWERS

- Spicy lettuce substitute
- Garnish

ROSEMARY

- Soups & stews
- Tomato-based dishes
- Baked potatoes
- Most vegetables

CRUSHED RED PEPPER FLAKES

- Soups & stews
- Salads
- Stir-fried foods
- Thai dishes

TURMERIC

- East Indian dishes
- Tofu dishes

Herb Enhancers

Possible Uses   "**My Favorite Uses**"

THYME

ᨭ Soups & stews

ᨭ Rice dishes

ᨭ Most vegetables

BAY LEAVES (BAY LAUREL)

ᨭ Soups & stews

BASIL

ᨭ Almost all tomato-based
   dishes

ᨭ Soups & stews

ᨭ Most vegetables

CAYENNE PEPPER

ᨭ Mexican and Thai dishes

ᨭ When you want added "heat"

ᨭ Excellent sprinkled in
   socks to warm your feet!

CARDAMOM

ᨭ Soups, stews & sauces

ᨭ East Indian dishes

CORIANDER (FINELY GROUND)

ᨭ Yam or pumpkin pie

ᨭ Thai dishes

Herb Enhancers

Possible Uses   "**My Favorite Uses**"

CORIANDER (WHOLE POD)

ᨭ East Indian dishes

CUMIN

ᨭ East Indian and Mexican dishes

ᨭ Stews & chili

ᨭ Rice dishes

ᨭ Vegetables

CURRY (MAKE YOUR OWN—SEE PAGE 122)

ᨭ East Indian dishes

CHIVES, GARLIC OR ONION

ᨭ Potatoes & squash

ᨭ Sprinkled in salads

CHILI POWDER

ᨭ Mexican dishes

ᨭ Tofu dishes

ᨭ Chili & stews

CELERY SEED

ᨭ Salads, especially potato or coleslaw

ᨭ Dips and appetizers

CILANTRO

ᨭ Salsa & other Mexican dishes

ᨭ East Indian dishes

NUTS

Nuts are excellent to keep on hand as key ingredients, garnishes, and toppings. If you're concerned about a deficiency of protein in your diet, please know that legumes and nuts are the richest source of protein among foods of plant origin. Because they're a concentrated food, however, a little goes a long way. Eat them in moderation.

Whenever possible, use raw nuts rather than roasted ones. Not only are they much easier to digest, but they still have precious enzymes that are lost in the roasting process. Keep all nuts refrigerated or frozen.

Almonds

Almonds contain the highest amount of protein of any nut: 84 grams of the highest quality protein per pound. They're excellent for teeth and bones; abundant in phosphorus and iron; high in calcium, potassium, and niacin. They're also a ready source of thiamin (B1), and riboflavin (B2). High in unsaturated fat (read *energy*) and easy to pack, they're the ideal snack item to carry with you on a plane when traveling, or when you're hiking or backpacking.

Almonds are a perfect addition when used sliced as a garnish or topping, or as a filler in a loaf. They add that elegant final touch to salads, gravies, Asian dishes, and desserts. Consider *almond butter* as a refreshing alternative to peanut butter. In his book *The Sleeping Prophet*, Edgar Cayce recommended eating ten raw almonds every day as a cancer preventative. Almonds

are the only nuts that alkalize the blood; all others acidify. They are ideal for building an alkaline reserve for acid-forming conditions such as stress, lack of exercise, and poor dietary habits.

Cashews

Cashews are a good source of vitamin D, iron, thiamine (B1), and protein. They're also high in fat, versatile, and an excellent substitute for vegetable oil when mixed in a blender with water (1/4 cup cashews to 1 cup water).

Peanuts

The peanut is actually a legume, but it's treated like a nut. It's a good source of niacin, B vitamins, calcium, and carbohydrates. When buying peanut oil, peanut butter, or any other peanut product, make sure to buy organic. Peanuts and cotton crops are typically rotated on the same land, with cotton being the most highly sprayed cultivated crop in this country. Peanuts are easily contaminated and can become carcinogenic. (*Healing with Whole Foods*, Paul Pitchford, 1993.) Avoid peanut butter that's hydrogenated. In fact, avoid hydrogenated anything, since altered fat substances are linked with the occurrence of cancers.

Walnuts, English or Black

An excellent source of phosphorous, calcium, and unsaturated fatty acids, walnuts are easy to carry with you to eat raw. They're also fantastic as the key ingredient in casserole dishes and desserts.

Baked Acorn Squash, see page 77

LEGUMES

Split Peas, Yellow or Green

I've found that yellow and green split peas taste enough alike to use them interchangeably. I buy about three or four cups of each kind and store them in quart-size glass canning jars, as they add richness to the color scheme of my pantry. I also use color as the deciding factor when I select them for soups or other dishes. Excellent for soup, sandwich spreads, and **Split Pea Daal** (see pg. 28), an East Indian dish that resembles American split pea soup, but whose flavor is distinctly different.

Pinto Beans

Pinto beans are perfect for making refried beans. They're inexpensive and easy to prepare. Rinse them well, picking through them carefully for stones and thorns.

Black Beans

Black beans are excellent by themselves or in vegetable stews, soups, dips. They have a rich, exciting flavor.

Lentils

Lentils are sumptuous in chili, soups, and casseroles.

Navy Beans

Navy beans are exceptional in soups of all kinds and are especially well suited for baked beans.

Kidney Beans

Kidney beans are excellent cooked, chilled, and marinated. They're great as the main ingredient in chili and are indispensable in minestrone, the "Queen of Soups."

SEEDS

Hulled Sesame Seeds

Hulled sesame seeds are great in salads, salad dressings, gravies, and desserts. They're the basis of tahini, which can be used in a number of ways. They're an excellent source of phosphorus, with one cup of sesame seeds containing a whopping 1,125 mg. of calcium. They're also high in unsaturated oils and lecithin, and rich in valuable amino acids, especially methionine, which is difficult to find in most foods. Blood cholesterol drops when this amino acid is present.

Olives

Olives, like nuts, are excellent providers of beneficial unsaturated oils, and quite versatile in the diet. If you're accustomed to buying regular black or green olives, for a taste treat you might consider picking up a jar of Greek calamata olives. They're distinctly different and perfectly marvelous.

Sunflower Seeds

Use sunflower seeds raw. They're an excellent source of vitamin D, which is unusual for a plant food. Ounce for ounce, they contain more protein than meat, eggs, or cheese. They also contain these minerals: calcium, magnesium, silicon, fluorine, and phosphorus, which are essential for strong bones and teeth. Sunflower seeds are said to contain all the essential nutrients to life. They're also a tasty addition to sandwiches, cereals, cookies, and salads, and delicious when eaten as a snack food.

GRAINS

Long-Grain Brown Rice

This type of rice is best used for almost all dishes calling for brown rice. When cooked according to directions, it separates into single grains and is moist but not sticky. It's also great in casseroles, side dishes, or just by itself with a little shake of tamari.

Short-Grain Brown Rice

Because it cooks up moist and the grains stick together somewhat, it is also called sticky rice and is ideal for making vegetable sushi.

Basmati Rice

This rice has a luscious nutty flavor that adds a dramatic taste to foods. It's especially tantalizing when it accompanies stir-fried dishes. "Basmati rice is good for regular use because it is parboiled before it is polished. This parboiling drives the vitamins and minerals deep into the grain so that only small amounts are lost during the milling process." (Robert Svoboda, *Your Ayurvedic*

Constitution.) A white rice, basmati cooks in only 15 to 20 minutes.

Rolled Oats

Rolled oats are one of the most overlooked building blocks of a sound, toxin-free, and healthful diet. It's the perfect quick-food for a filling breakfast or as a delicious filler in casseroles. It also makes fantastic burgers and is the basic ingredient of most granolas. Rolled oats are perhaps the only cereal that retain the germ of the grain after they're milled. When combined properly, they're one of the finest disease-prevention foods we have. The biochemical breakdown is astounding. An unrefined carbohydrate with high fiber content, rolled oats contain protein, potassium, calcium, magnesium, and phosphorous; and traces of sodium, sulphur, chlorine, fluorine, iodine, and ash.

Wheat Flakes

This yummy breakfast cereal takes about 40 minutes to cook. It's perfect on a cold morning when you have extra time and want a leisurely breakfast. Wheat flakes are available in bulk at health-food stores.

Barley

Barley is the ideal ingredient for homemade soup. It transforms a mere vegetable soup into a warm and filling meal.

Couscous

Couscous is not really a grain, but rather a combination

of semolina, flour, water, and salt. It cooks in 5 minutes and is a great rice substitute.

Quinoa

Pronounced "KEEN-wah," this grain was cultivated and used as a staple by the ancient Incas of South America. It has been grown in the United States since the mid-1980s. A complete protein with a light nutty flavor, it combines easily with a variety of vegetables, and it cooks in 15 to 20 minutes. A charming feature is that once quinoa is cooked, each grain is surrounded with a lucent halo.

One evening at table when my daughter Sara was about seven years old, she held up a forkful of quinoa to the light and asked, "Is this what angel food cake is made of?"

BASIC KITCHEN EQUIPMENT

Cutlery

Because many foods in the vegetarian diet are raw and require chopping, a sharp vegetable cleaver and a cutting board are basic tools. My preference for a knife or cleaver blade is either carbon steel or high-quality stainless steel.

Juicer

Although there are many fine juicers on the market today, the Champion is the only one I'm aware of that has the kind of centrifugal action that purées frozen fruit and juices melons—a must for the real fruit lover who enjoys unique juices and desserts and prefers a minimum of fat intake. With the Champion, you can make a dessert that resembles soft ice cream, yet is composed of only frozen fruit. As for durability, I bought mine used in 1975, and it's still going strong.

Blender

The blender is the perfect tool for mixing just about anything: beverages, gravies, sauces, salad dressings, mayonnaise, and vegetables.

Food Processor

A food processor is not a must, but it certainly saves time when chopping, dicing, and grating large amounts of vegetables or fruits.

Pots & Pans

No aluminum, ever! I find that good old-fashioned cast iron is the best kind of skillet and soup kettle to use, and enamelware or stainless steel makes for the most efficient pots and pans. I tried the heavy glassware but found that most foods stuck to the bottom and the pans were difficult to clean. They also break.

Stainless-Steel Wok

A stainless-steel wok makes all the difference when you stir-fry. Be sure you don't get aluminum; they're usually the ones on sale. Those made of stainless steel may cost a little more, but they're not harmful to your health and last forever.

Avo-Reuben Sandwich, see page 130

Vegetable Steamer

Vegetable steamers come in two pretty standard versions. The first is a little portable stainless-steel steaming tray that folds up like a flower. It's used by placing it in a saucepan in which you put water, and it holds about four cups of vegetables. The second is called a corn pot, which is a pot within a pot; the inner pot has holes to allow the steam through and can hold up to four medium artichokes.

Lettuce Spinner

Being a cooking professional, my daughter Sara considers this a little frivolous, but I would be lost without mine. This is a plastic bowl-within-a-bowl with a lid and handle to spin the inner bowl. It dries the lettuce, spinach, or other greens in seconds.

Miscellaneous

❖ A **vegetable brush** with natural bristles is tremendous for washing/scrubbing vegetables. It can be kept near the sink for convenience.

❖ Friends laugh when they see my wooden **cutting board** for the first time; then they go home and do theirs the same way. I used a permanent marker to write NO ONIONS on the top edge of one side, and ONIONS OKAY on the other.

❖ **Kitchen shears** come in handy. I use them especially for snipping off the thorns on artichoke leaves. The handle of most kitchen shears doubles as an opener for bottles or small jars, with grooves to hold jar and bottle caps while you twist.

Other than that, your usual basic kitchen tools work well with anything you may prepare.

ONE LAST WORD

Cooking in the kitchen is an opportunity for the food preparer to share more than just a sumptuous casserole, salad, or dessert. The quality of energy the cook puts into the food is as vital as the clean hands and quality of ingredients. You might look at it as nutrition on a higher level. The attitude of the cook automatically spills into the preparation of the meal.

Cooking is an opportunity to bless those whom you love—not only with the food you prepare, but also with the heartfelt energy you put into it. Every chop, dice, stir, or mix creates a subtle ingredient. Once the meal is served, you might even consider placing your hands silently on either side of your plate (or holding hands around the table), closing your eyes, then reaching into your heart to express gratitude.

As a family, we always said grace before meals. The last phrase before the "Amen" was, *"Dear God, please bless everyone who was in any way responsible for getting this food to our table"*—a loving reminder to us that our family was much larger than just the ten of us.

Main Dishes

"I give you every seed-bearing plant on the earth
and every tree which has seed-bearing fruit to be your food."

— Genesis 1:29

TOSTADAS ELEGANTE, SEE PAGE 33

Beans & Legumes

TIPS & SHORTCUTS

❖ Always pick through beans and legumes before cooking, and rinse them well. Discard any odd-looking ones.

❖ Cook in a large pot, keeping beans or legumes covered with water during cooking.

❖ Cover, but tilt the lid a bit when reducing the heat from a high boil to a simmer, so that the beans don't boil over.

❖ Soaking beans overnight shortens cooking time. When you cook beans that have been soaked, discard the water they've been soaking in and replace with fresh water before you begin cooking; this reduces the risk of the beans producing intestinal gas.

❖ When you soak soy beans, put them in the refrigerator to soak, as they may begin to ferment at room temperature.

❖ One cup dry beans equals about 2¹/₂ cups cooked.

❖ Don't add salt or oil to beans until after they're cooked.

COOKING CHART, BEANS

One Cup [Dry]	Soak	Water	Cook Time
Black	Overnight	4 cups	3 hours
Kidney	No need	3 cups	2 hours
Lentils	No need	3 cups	45 minutes
Navy beans	No need	3 cups	90 minutes
Pintos	No need	3 cups	90 minutes
Soy	Overnight in refrigerator	4 cups	3¹/₂ hours
Split peas	No need	3 cups	45 minutes
1 cup dry beans yields about 2¹/₂ cups cooked beans.			

BASIC BEANS FOR FILLING TOSTADAS, ENCHILADAS & BURRITOS

You might want to bookmark this recipe, as it is basic to many dishes.

1¹/₂ cups dry beans (pintos are best for authentic flavor)
4 cups water
Cook until done, about 90 minutes
Drain most of the remaining liquid
   (or use canned pinto beans)

ADD:
1 teaspoon sea salt (or to taste)

MASH BEANS, THEN ADD:
1 onion, minced
¹/₂ bell pepper, chopped
¹/₃ cup salsa (see pg. 118 to make your own)

SPLIT PEA DAAL

This is an East Indian dish that's truly marvelous. Serve with steaming hot rice and a green vegetable of your choice with chutney as a condiment. Yummm!

- **PREPARATION TIME: 20 minutes**
- **COOKING TIME: 40 minutes**
- **SERVES: 4**

1 cup split peas, yellow or green
3 cups water
1 cup string beans, cut (1")
1 cup cubed (1") summer squash
Sea salt to taste
¹/₄ cup coconut flakes, unsweetened
1 teaspoon cumin (or more, to taste)
¹/₂ teaspoon brown sugar
¹/₂ teaspoon lemon juice
1 Tablespoon **Ghee** (see pg. 40)

Cook split peas 20 minutes in water. Add remaining ingredients and simmer an additional 20 minutes. That's it!

See picture, page 30

VIMALA'S HOLIDAY NUT LOAF

For a delectable holiday menu, serve with the green salad of your choice, mushroom gravy, baked yams or mashed potatoes with carrot purée, peas with tiny onions, and cranberry sauce. For dessert, serve **Holiday Mince Pie** *(see pg. 161),* **Yam Pie** *(see pg. 162), or* **Cranberry Crisp with Sweet Whipped Tofu Topping** *(see pg. 169).*

- **PREPARATION TIME: 10 minutes (using food processor)**
- **BAKING TIME: 25 minutes**
- **SERVES: 6–8**

2 medium golden onions, minced

3 cloves garlic, minced

1/2 cup fresh parsley, chopped

4 cups walnuts, finely ground

2 Tablespoons tahini

3 cups soft bread crumbs

1/2 to 1 cup tomato juice

1 teaspoon salt

A food processor minces nuts and vegetables finely —and quickly.

Preheat oven to 350°. Sauté all vegetables together. Combine all ingredients in a mixing bowl, using enough tomato juice to create loaf consistency. The tahini serves as a tasty binder to hold the ingredients together. Pack firmly into a 9" x 5" x 3" well-oiled non-aluminum loaf pan, and bake uncovered for 25–30 minutes. If the top begins to get too dark, lightly cover with aluminum foil.

Split Pea Daal, see page 28

CHINESE SPAGHETTI, SEE PAGE 32

CHINESE SPAGHETTI

*Goes well with a mixed-greens salad with **Sweet & Sour Dressing** (see pg. 112), served with baked or steamed sweet potatoes.*

- PREPARATION TIME: 20 minutes
- COOKING TIME: 35 minutes
- SERVES: 4

1 cup lentils, uncooked
3 cups water
1/4 cup tamari
1/4 cup honey
1/3 cup apple cider vinegar
1 1/2 teaspoons fresh gingerroot, peeled and grated
1/2 pound Udon noodles
1 Tablespoon sesame oil
1 clove garlic, minced
1 large carrot, grated
1/2 medium green bell pepper, chopped
2 bunches scallions, chopped (including healthy green tops)

Wash, rinse, and pick through lentils. Cook in water for 30 minutes. In a small jar, mix tamari, honey, vinegar, and ginger. Shake well and set aside. Cook the Udon noodles and drain. Heat a large skillet and add sesame oil. Sauté garlic and carrot, bell pepper and scallions, cooking just long enough for scallions to begin softening. Add cooked lentils to the sweet/sour mixture, simmering together for about 3–5 minutes.

Add the cooked Udon, simmering until just heated through.

❧

At the end of a very long day, I was rummaging through the cupboard wondering what to fix for dinner. Absentmindedly, I took out honey, tamari, Udon noodles, and a jar of lentils, then went to the refrigerator and pulled out a few carrots, scallions, a piece of gingerroot, and a bell pepper or two. Dazed and doubting, I put everything out on the counter, wondering how or if I could combine any of this into a meal.

One of the kids piped up, "I thought you said we were going to have spaghetti tonight," and another, "No we're supposed to have lentil soup." "But I want Chinese food!" said yet another.

I looked at the odds and ends spread out before me and answered, "Hmm. Okay. Trust me. You'll all get what you want. Now you go do your homework, and I'll do mine." This dish became a family favorite.

See picture, page 31

Tostadas Elegante

*A meal in itself! Serve with corn chips and salsa
on the side.*

- **PREPARATION TIME: 20 minutes**
- **COOKING TIME: 10 minutes**
- **SERVES: One tostada per person**

FOR EACH TOSTADA:

1 whole-wheat tortilla

1/4 cup refried beans

1/4 cup tomatoes, chopped

1 Tablespoon scallions, chopped (including green tops)

1 Tablespoon black olives, chopped

1 teaspoon **Mexican Salsa** (see pg. 118)

Several spinach leaves, torn

Several green leaf lettuce leaves, torn

3 or 4 avocado slices

Alfalfa-radish sprouts

5 (or more) shakes apple cider vinegar

In a dry skillet, warm tortilla over medium heat. Place on baking pan to assemble tostada. Heap beans in center of tortilla, then distribute tomatoes, scallions, and olives on top of them. Place lettuce and spinach over vegetables, then add avocado slices on top, arranging them attractively. Top with salsa. Tear shreds of sprouts over the top of all this. The fabulous finale is five or more (your taste dictates how many) good shakes of apple cider vinegar over the filling, just as it's being served. Flavor magic!

See picture, page 26

SARA'S CHILI SUPREME

Marvelous over steaming basmati rice, served with your favorite green salad, cornbread, and maybe even tofu hot dogs. Or serve over sprouted-wheat burger buns. A potluck favorite.

• **PREPARATION: Precook beans**
• **AFTER BEANS ARE COOKED: 20 minutes**
• **YIELD: 10 generous portions**

3 cups dry beans (pinto, kidney, or navy), cooked according
   to directions, or 8 cups cooked beans
2 cups onions, chopped
3 cups carrots, chopped
2 medium bell peppers, chopped
2 cups zucchini, chopped
One 8-ounce can green chilis, drained and diced
Two 28-ounce cans Roma tomatoes, whole, peeled
3 cloves garlic, minced (or 1 teaspoon garlic powder)
$1/2$ teaspoon black pepper, coarsely ground
1 teaspoon crushed red pepper (or more, to taste)
2 Tablespoons chili powder
1 teaspoon cumin
1 cup frozen tofu thawed, squeezed, and crumbled.

If you cook your own beans, add all ingredients during the last 30 minutes of cooking, breaking tomatoes apart with your hands. If you use canned or previously cooked beans, put them with above ingredients in a large pot and cook gently for 20 minutes—longer for the richest flavor.

See picture on next page

Sara's Chili Supreme

Magic Black Beans

Goes well with steaming hot rice, millet, or couscous.

Soak beans overnight
- **PREPARATION TIME: 10 minutes**
- **COOKING TIME: 2¹/₂ hours**
- **SERVES: 6**

2 cups black beans
2 quarts **Basic Broth** (see pg. 66)
1 bay leaf
1 bell pepper, chopped
1 golden onion, minced
2 cloves garlic, minced
2 Tablespoons sesame oil
2 Tablespoons apple cider vinegar
¹/₄ teaspoon ground coriander
Sea salt to taste

Drain the water the beans have soaked in and add broth. Cook beans in broth with a bay leaf for 2 hours. Once they're cooked, drain all but about 1 cup of the broth. Sauté bell pepper, onion, and garlic in sesame oil until almost soft, and add to beans. Sprinkle mixture with coriander and vinegar and mix well. Add salt to taste.

If you don't want beans two days in a row, make a black bean salsa with the leftovers by adding to **Jean-Marie's Mexican Salsa** (see pg. 118).

Rice

TIPS & SHORTCUTS

Rice comes in a variety of forms: long or short grain, white or brown, basmati or regular. It can be used for breakfast, lunch, or dinner, prepared simply, or adorned with gourmet touches. It tastes good in both hot and cold dishes and is one of the friendliest foods you can feed your body. As if that weren't enough, it's high in fiber, phosphorous, potassium, protein, carbohydrates, minerals, and the important family of B vitamins.

❖ Buy organic whenever possible.

❖ To help reduce the starch content, rinse rice before you cook it. Place it in a colander in the sink and run cold water through it or use a hand-held strainer.

❖ Use twice as much water as rice unless otherwise indicated.

❖ 1 cup dry equals $2^1/2$ cups cooked.

❖ For a pleasant taste variety, cook any rice with 1 vegetable bouillon cube to 2 cups water instead of plain water.

HOW TO COOK RICE AND BEANS

Use an enamel or stainless steel cooking pot. Bring water to a boil, add rice (or beans), cover, and reduce heat to simmer, tipping cover to avoid boil-over. Once the water is simmering, place lid on firmly. Simmer, covered, until done.

❖ **Beans**: Cooking time varies with the type of bean.

❖ **Rice**: 20 minutes for basmati rice, 40–45 minutes for brown rice, long or short grain, unless otherwise indicated.

ABOUT OTHER GRAINS

Experiment! Interchange couscous with quinoa, or millet with couscous, or couscous with rice, and discover subtle and exciting differences.

❖ **Couscous** is native to Morocco, Algeria, and Tunisia. It has a delicate flavor. Use 1 cup couscous to 1 cup water. Boil water, add couscous, stir, cover, and remove from heat. Let stand 5 minutes. That's all there is to it!

Phenomenal Rice Stuffing, see page 46

❖ **Quinoa** cooks in 15–20 minutes. Use 2 cups water to one cup quinoa. One cup dry equals 5 cups cooked.

❖ **Millet** cooks in about 12 minutes. Use 3 cups water to 1 cup millet. Bring to a boil, then simmer, covered, for 12 minutes. Remove from heat and let sit uncovered for another 15 minutes. This method prevents the mushy consistency that can occur from overcooking.

SESAME RICE

*Its subtle flavor tastes as though the rice took hours to prepare. Incredible served with lightly steamed broccoli with **Super Quick Sesame Dressing** (see pg. 113).*

- **PREPARATION TIME: 10 minutes**
- **COOKING TIME FOR WHITE RICE: 20 minutes**
- **COOKING TIME FOR BROWN RICE: 45 minutes**
- **SERVES: 3**

2 cups water
1 cup rice
2 Tablespoons tamari
2 Tablespoons toasted sesame seeds
$1/2$ teaspoon fresh gingerroot, peeled and grated

Cook rice. Five minutes before the rice is done, stir in tamari, sesame seeds, and grated ginger. Leave uncovered over lowest heat for balance of cooking time.

KITCHARI WITH GHEE

A tantalizing dish from India.

This is an East Indian dish that almost everyone loves. A common response by first-time tasters is to break into a huge grin with their first bite. "What is this?" It goes beautifully with lightly steamed Swiss chard, kale, or your favorite leafy green vegetable. An all-greens raw salad is a lovely accompaniment.

- SOAK MUNG DAAL: 4–5 hours or overnight
- PREPARATION TIME: 20 minutes
- COOKING TIME: 20–25 minutes
- YIELD: 8 servings

1 cup yellow mung daal (or split peas if daal
   is not available)
1 cup basmati rice
2" piece of fresh gingerroot, peeled and diced
1/2 cup shredded coconut, unsweetened
1 generous-size bunch cilantro leaves, chopped
3/4 cup water
1/4 cup **Ghee** (make your own—see next page)
1 Tablespoon turmeric
1/2 teaspoon salt
3 cups water

Rinse daal well, then soak 4–5 hours, or overnight in cold water. Drain and rinse before using. Put ginger, coconut, cilantro, turmeric, salt, and 3/4 cup water in blender until they're of a coarse consistency. Heat the ghee in a large saucepan and add the blended ingredients. Rinse the rice several times, then add daal and rice to saucepan with the 3 cups water. Bring to boil, cover, turn to simmer, and cook for 20–25 minutes.

❧

INFO ON GHEE

WHAT IS GHEE?

You're probably asking, "Since ghee is clarified butter, why do you use it, since you use no other animal-based product?" I use ghee not only because it has an incredible taste, but also because, when made from butter untouched by pesticides or hormonal additives, it is healing for the body. First of all—what is it?

Ghee is butter with the milk solids removed. It's an ancient food, considered sacred in some cultures, and is a source of healing, especially of the liver. King Tutankhamen died in Egypt in about 1350 B.C. When his burial site was discovered by Howard Carter in 1922, ghee was found, having been left as an offering to the gods. After 3,272 years, it was still pure and unspoiled.

HOW IT'S USED

In India, ghee is used extensively, and it's prescribed as a remedy in Ayurvedic medicine to nourish the liver, the nervous system, and the brain. It also provides relief for fevers and infections.

I'm sure that the tradition of dipping artichoke leaves in ghee stemmed from the fact that both artichokes and ghee are healing to the liver. As a teenager, my rigorously healthy body succumbed to hepatitis—something about burning the candle at both ends. When I discovered the healing properties of artichokes, I made it a point to eat one artichoke a week. Has it helped? I have no way of knowing. I do know, however, that I'm extraordinarily healthy, and besides, eating artichokes is a pleasurable habit!

HOW TO MAKE IT

Use one pound unsalted butter (this will reduce to a little less than one pound of ghee). In a large skillet, on a low-medium setting, slowly simmer one pound unsalted butter.

As the butter bubbles, keep scooping off the white foam that forms on the top; these are the milk solids. After about 12–15 minutes, the ghee will suddenly begin to make a crackling noise—the same sound heard when water hits hot oil. Immediately remove it from the heat. Skim off any remaining foam. After about 5 minutes, pour the ghee into a perfectly dry, sterile glass container, and store at room temperature.

As you will discover, ghee has an indescribably sweet taste, one of those magical flavors in the kitchen. It can be used on vegetables, toast, and with any other food you might ordinarily use butter for. I store mine in a lovely glass jar in the cupboard.

It's extremely important to buy butter that comes from vegetarian cows. Creutzfeldt-Jakob (Mad Cow) Disease, and Foot and Mouth Disease are a concern here. Ascertain that the cows from which your butter comes are not injected with Bovine Growth Hormone (rBGH), and that they've been fed organically grown grain. Although cows are natural vegetarians, factory-farm cows are often fed the remnants of other animals and sawdust as a filler in their grain. What grain they do receive has often been heavily sprayed with pesticides. Play it safe. Go organic. See the Resources section for more information.

AVOCADO SHIITAKE SUSHI

This is so simple to prepare, and may easily become a quick-fix staple in your diet! An energy food, it makes a hearty breakfast, a filling snack, or an extraordinary appetizer.

- **PREPARATION (WITH COOKED RICE): 10 minutes**
- **FOR RICE PREPARATION, ADD: 20 minutes**
- **SERVES: 4**

3 cups cooked rice, or
3/4 cup uncooked basmati rice
2 1/2 cups water
4 sheets nori*
1 ripe avocado
2 shiitake mushrooms
1/2 cup tamari
1 teaspoon Spike®

Prepare rice. Cover dried mushrooms with hot water and soak for 10 minutes. Place one sheet of nori on a smooth surface. Spread 3/4 cup rice evenly over the nori, pressing it down slightly. Sprinkle lightly with 2 Tablespoons tamari. Divide avocado into four even sections, one for each roll. Slice one section very thin and place along the edge of the rice, about 1" wide. Sprinkle avocados with 1/4 teaspoon Spike®. Slice soft mushrooms into thin strips and place on avocados. Roll up from avocado edge, making one long tube-shape. Cut into 1" slices and serve. Repeat for remaining ingredients. Especially flavorful when served with slices of pickled ginger.

*Nori (*porphyra tenera*) is a magical food. It is 48% protein and decreases cholesterol, lowers high blood pressure, aids in digestion, helps maintain a hormonal balance in the body, and is rich in vitamins A, B1, and niacin. Besides that, it tastes marvelous! I often munch it as a snack.

See picture on next page

AVOCADO SHIITAKE SUSHI

MEXICAN RICE

*This goes beautifully with any Mexican dish. It's an especially nice complement to **Sara's Mexican Salad** (see pg. 104).*

- **PREPARATION TIME: 10 minutes**
- **COOKING TIME FOR WHITE RICE: 20 minutes**
- **COOKING TIME FOR BROWN RICE: 40 minutes**
- **SERVES: 4**

1 Tablespoon sesame oil
1 clove garlic, minced
1 cup uncooked rice
1 cup tomato sauce
2 cups boiling water
1 teaspoon sea salt
1 teaspoon cumin
1 teaspoon chili powder

Sauté garlic in oil in a heavy skillet. Add uncooked rice, and roast until golden. Add remaining ingredients. Bring to a boil. Stir to mix. Immediately cover and simmer for 40 minutes (brown rice), or 20 minutes (basmati).

RICE PILAF

This could easily become a family favorite. The flavors blend especially well with baked yellow squash that has been sprinkled with nutmeg and a shake or two of garlic powder. Raw or slightly steamed sweet peas add the finishing touch. Scintillating!

- **PREPARATION TIME: 20 minutes**
  (10 minutes or less, using food processor)
- **COOKING TIME: 30 minutes**
- **SERVES: 6**

1 Tablespoon toasted sesame oil
1/2 cup bell pepper, minced
1/2 cup onion, minced
1/2 cup celery, minced
1 cup uncooked rice
1 cup tomatoes, chopped
2 cups vegetable bouillon broth
1 1/2 teaspoons sea salt
1/4 teaspoon black pepper, coarsely ground
1/2 teaspoon powdered oregano (or 1 Tablespoon fresh, chopped)

In a 10" or 12" cast-iron skillet, sauté vegetables in oil for about 3 minutes. Add rice, tomatoes, broth, herbs, and spices. Bring to gentle boil, turn heat to low, and cover. Simmer for 30 minutes.

JOOK A.K.A. CONGEE A.K.A. CHINESE CHICKEN SOUP!

Of all the foods I've ever tasted or prepared, this is my very favorite, with no competitors even close. It's what I prepare when I go into the kitchen, look around, and find that nothing looks good. It's what I prepare when my stomach is just a little off. It's what I prepare when I want to treat myself to something special. It's what I prepare when I've been stressed and need to get back in my body—that is, be centered. Jook always makes me feel good—physically, mentally, spiritually, and emotionally.

- **PREPARATION TIME: 3 minutes**
- **COOKING TIME: 1 to 4 hours—you choose**
- **SERVES: 3**

1 cup basmati rice
6 cups water (or more, if you prefer)

Rinse rice under cold running water, place in saucepan (or crockpot), add water, and bring to a boil. Turn heat as low as possible, cover pot, and simmer anywhere from 1–4 hours, depending on the consistency desired. Jook is often cooked until it's of a porridge consistency, so add more water if you like.

Eat it plain or, if you choose, add:

1/2 cup yams, thinly sliced, or
1/2 cup of your favorite beans, or
1 cup leafy green vegetable: chard, bok choy, kale, broccoli
thinly sliced, or any other chopped vegetable of your choosing

Cook until of desired consistency.

Jook, also called *congee* or *hsi-fan* (rice water) is to the Chinese what chicken soup is to someone of Jewish heritage. It's considered a comfort food in all of China. In the North, it's often prepared with yams or beans. The Fountain Court Restaurant on Clement Street in San Francisco serves their jook with cooked yams—the only Chinese restaurant I know of in this city that features this dish on their dinner menu.

Nutritionally, this simple rice porridge strengthens the spleen-pancreas digestive center, tonifies the blood, balances the qi energy, and cools the body. Not only that, it's extremely beneficial for nursing mothers, as it will not only nourish them, but increase their milk supply. All this with a little rice and water!

PHENOMENAL RICE STUFFING

Excellent for any dinner, but especially well suited for your holiday menu. You'll be asked for this recipe again and again.

- **PREPARATION TIME: 20 minutes**
  (10 minutes using food processor)
- **BAKING TIME: 20 minutes**
- **SERVES: 6**

2 Tablespoons sesame oil
4 cups cooked white basmati rice
1/2 cup walnuts, broken
1/4 cup walnuts, finely ground
1 medium bell pepper, diced
1/2 cup celery, diced
1 medium onion, minced
2 Tablespoons tamari
1/2 cup raisins
2 teaspoons cumin (or more, to taste)
1/4 teaspoon black pepper, coarsely ground

In a large skillet, sauté onion, bell pepper, and celery 5 minutes. Add rice and remaining ingredients. Stir until well mixed and heated through. Place in oiled glass or ceramic casserole dish and bake for 20 minutes.

When I was just becoming a vegetarian I hated to give up this recipe but thought I would have to because we had made it with sausage. In my family's meat-eating days, it had been our holiday turkey stuffing, so I equated it with both sausage and turkey. One afternoon I decided to experiment and make it without the sausage to see what it would taste like. I had most of the ingredients out on the counter, and in a flash of panic, I looked from the rice to the parsley to the walnuts and muttered aloud, "Oh, no! What am I going to stuff?" My daughter Stephanie happened to be walking by, heard me, and without missing a beat responded, "Hey, Mom, try a bell pepper!" And so it was . . .

See picture, page 38

Pasta (& Sauces)

TIPS & SHORTCUTS

❖ Buy sesame, whole-wheat, or artichoke pasta whenever possible. The flavor is richly different from the common enriched-wheat pasta. The colors liven up the appearance of the meal, and the nutritional value is far superior.

❖ Use 2¹/₂ cups sauce for 1 pound pasta.

❖ My daughter Sara taught me how to cook pasta so that it doesn't clump up and get gooey, but remains single-stranded and won't have a starchy residue. Her advice:

  ❖ Boil water. Just before you add the pasta, add ¹/₂ teaspoon extra virgin olive oil to the water.

❖ Once the pasta is cooked, drain it in a colander and rinse. If you're not serving it right away, rinse it with cold water. Once you're ready to serve, add sauce to a nonstick sauté pan to get it hot, then add the pasta.

❖ If you're serving it right away, rinse with hot water and pour sauce immediately over the pasta.

❖ While the pasta is cooking, you may want to poke around at it gently now and again. A chopstick works fine, and is far less intrusive than a fork.

SPAGHETTI CASSEROLE

*This is a simple dish to prepare, and is an instant hearty dinner for hungry teens and friends. Let them have the kitchen for this one and do it themselves. Perfect with your favorite green salad, **No-Oil Italian Dressing** (see pg. 112), and garlic bread.*

- **PREPARATION TIME: 10–15 minutes**
- **BAKING TIME: 20 minutes**
- **SERVES: 6–8**

4 medium tomatoes, chopped
One 15-ounce can tomato sauce
One 15-ounce can whole black olives, pitted
1 medium onion, minced
4 cloves garlic, minced
1/2 cup bell pepper, chopped
1 teaspoon dried basil
1/2 teaspoon dried oregano
1 cup mushrooms, sliced
Pinch cayenne pepper
1 pound vermicelli

Preheat oven to 350°. Place all ingredients except vermicelli in a 2-quart saucepan and cook over low to medium heat until onions are somewhat soft. Cook spaghetti according to package directions. Mix sauce and spaghetti together, and place in a 2-quart casserole dish. Bake covered for 20 minutes.

RATATOUILLE

*By transforming this French vegetable dish into a sauce, it becomes a magical accompaniment to any kind of pasta. Toss a mixture of raw salad greens, alfalfa sprouts, and slices of cucumber and mushrooms, sprinkle with **Vinaigrette Dressing** (see pg. 110), and your meal is complete.*

- **PREPARATION TIME: 15 minutes**
- **COOKING TIME: 25 minutes**
- **SERVES: 4**

1 Tablespoon extra virgin olive oil
1 medium onion, chopped
2 cloves garlic, chopped
1 small green bell pepper, chopped (1/2")
6 Roma tomatoes, stemmed and chopped
1 cup eggplant, peeled and cubed (1")
1 cup zucchini, cubed (1")
1 Tablespoon tomato paste
1 teaspoon dried oregano
1 teaspoon dried basil
1 teaspoon brown sugar
1 1/2 teaspoons sea salt, or to taste

In a skillet, heat oil, add onion and garlic, and sauté 5 minutes. Add vegetables, sauté 5 minutes, then stir in remaining ingredients. Spin half the vegetables in the blender, then add them back into the vegetables in the skillet. Simmer about 15 minutes.

BASIC MARINARA SAUCE

This goes with or over any Italian pasta dish. The longer this sauce simmers, the better it tastes.

- **PREPARATION TIME: 10 minutes**
- **COOKING TIME: 20 minutes**
- **SERVES: 4–6**

1 Tablespoon extra virgin olive oil
1 medium onion, minced
3 cloves garlic, minced
4 mushrooms, sliced
1 green bell pepper, chopped
One 28-ounce can whole Roma tomatoes
6 fresh basil leaves, finely chopped
   (or 1 teaspoon dried leaves)
1 bay leaf, broken in half
3 Tablespoons tomato paste
1 Tablespoon brown sugar
1 teaspoon dried marjoram
$1/2$ teaspoon sea salt
Pinch cinnamon

Heat oil in a 2-quart saucepan over medium heat. Add onions and garlic and sauté 2–3 minutes. Add remaining ingredients, breaking up the tomatoes with your hands. Cover and simmer for 15 minutes or longer. Use with your favorite pasta recipe.

NUTSO PESTO

This recipe has an unusual flavor and will have hearty diners singing your praises. It goes especially well with **Tomato Salad** *(see pg. 102) and garlic sourdough bread.*

- **PREPARATION TIME: 20 minutes**
- **SERVES: 4**

1 cup fresh basil, finely shredded and packed in a cup
$1/4$ cup fresh parsley, snipped or chopped
$1/2$ cup walnuts, well chopped
$1/4$ cup black olives, pitted and sliced
3 Tablespoons extra virgin olive oil
2 cloves garlic, minced
4 cups spinach fettuccine

Combine all ingredients except fettuccine in a blender. Mix to the consistency of a chunky paste. Cook fettuccine according to package directions. Toss hot fettuccine with the pesto in a warmed bowl, and serve immediately.

ZUCCHINI & BASIL PESTO

*Excellent served with your favorite green salad tossed with **No-Oil Tahini Dressing** (see pg. 113). French or sourdough bread completes this taste treat. The common response is: "May I have seconds?"*

- **PREPARATION TIME: 20 minutes**
- **COOKING TIME: 7 minutes**
- **SERVES: 6**

2 pounds medium zucchini

2 teaspoons sea salt

1/2 cup fresh basil leaves, finely shredded and tightly packed in a cup

2 Tablespoons extra virgin olive oil

4 medium garlic cloves, chopped

1 pound angel hair pasta

1/4 teaspoon black pepper, freshly ground

Grate zucchini into a mixing bowl. Toss with sea salt, mixing well. Let mixture sit for 10 minutes as you prepare other ingredients. Pick up zucchini by the handful and squeeze tightly to extract as much water as possible. Put squeezed zucchini in bowl with shredded basil, and toss together. In a 10" or 12" skillet, heat oil and sauté garlic over moderate heat. As soon as the garlic sizzles, add the zucchini-basil mixture and sauté until the zucchini begins to turn golden, about 5–7 minutes. Spoon over cooked angel hair pasta, and twist a few sprinkles of black pepper over the top.

See picture on next page

Zucchini & Basil Pesto

Tofu

WHAT IT IS AND HOW TO USE IT

In my early days as a vegetarian, tofu was an obstacle I was not only going to overcome, but master. White, flavorless, with an odd texture; but low fat, and full of protein and essential B vitamins—I had been told it was exceedingly nutritious and easy to combine into healthful meals. But how would I use it?

Once I brought it home and put it in the refrigerator, that's where it stayed. "Now that I've bought it, what do I do with it?" I asked myself.

That little container with contents of incredible health potential remained on the shelf day after day. Then one morning I looked at it and realized that the water it was packed in, once clear, had become murky and yellowish, and the tofu itself had an indescribable appearance, a little slimy around the edges and not at all pleasant. And out it went. I searched cookbooks for appetizing recipes, but found not a one.

One day in complete frustration, I realized that my kitchen would have to become a tofu laboratory. From that day on, the results were sometimes rewarding and at other times downright discouraging. Now and again, they were awfully funny. I disguised the tofu by trying to have it taste like meat. There were eight children, remember, and I had gone cold turkey (excuse the expression) into a non-meat diet. I gave the dishes I prepared clever little names when they reached the table in an attempt to sidetrack any prejudices.

"Almost-Chicken Cacciatore," was the one disaster all the children still remember renaming "Chicken Yuk." It must have been pretty bad.

Sad to say, it was only one of my many tofu disasters. With relentless determination, I kept experimenting, and little by little, it began to pay off. Somehow we all survived the tofu trauma, with the end result being countless creative recipes from main dishes to desserts.

I learned the hard way that tofu has an elegance all its own, and I began to create meals to reflect this unique quality. After a while, it no longer reached the table in clandestine attire. It was, plain and simple, tofu: Asian, Mexican, or down-home American, and accepted more and more with praise. When my children's school friends began to ask for my recipes to give to their moms, I knew I had scored.

A few suggestions: Because tofu is so quick and easy to prepare, and is by far the most versatile and flexible food you can imagine, I strongly recommend always having one pound on standby in the refrigerator and one in the freezer. Because it has no appreciable flavor of its own, it blends agreeably with many types of foods. It has saved the day many a time for me when unexpected guests have arrived.

NUTRITIONAL VALUE

Nutritionally, tofu has the lowest ratio of calories to protein found in any known plant food. It's unique among high-protein foods because it's not only low in calories and saturated fats, but, being non-animal based, is entirely free of cholesterol. Although tofu is high in protein, unlike most high-protein foods that are acid-forming, tofu has an alkaline composition that is user-friendly. When you read the label on a tofu package, look for *nigari* (another name for *bittern*) as a preservative. Nigari is the liquid left after natural sea salt is extracted from seawater. It's high in minerals and complements tofu as a natural preservative.

KINDS OF TOFU

Silken

Japanese in origin, silken tofu has a very refined, silken texture. I use it for **Tofu Mayonnaise** (see pg. 122), sour cream, or whipped cream because of the texture. It comes in a small box and can be stored on the cupboard shelf.

Firm

Chinese in origin, firm tofu comes in solid blocks or slices about $1^1/_2$" thick in one-pound containers. Any recipe that calls for frozen tofu means firm tofu that has been cut into 1" cubes and frozen about 6–8 hours. Silken or Soft are just too soft.

Soft

I've never figured out a use for soft tofu because it's so watery. It has the consistency of very wet cottage cheese, and being a texture-conscious person, I don't use it because I find the texture disagreeable.

Frozen

Once tofu is frozen, the texture changes dramatically. It becomes porous and resembles a soft honeycomb; thawed, it becomes marvelously chewy, which often comforts meat-eaters because of its textural similarity to ground meat. It's especially great in tomato-based dishes such as **Basic Marinara Sauce** (see pg. 49) or **Tofu-chiladas** (see pg. 58). Because it's extremely absorbent, it soaks up marinades beautifully.

Shredded

Use firm or extra firm tofu, blotted and squeezed. Shred on a hand grater just as you would a carrot for carrot-raisin salad.

Marinated

Marinate tofu in glass, enamel, or stainless-steel flat pans. Turn pieces several times, spooning marinade over the pieces. Always marinate in the refrigerator.

If you'd like to know more about the history and use of the magnificent soybean, there's an exceedingly thorough and well-written article in the July 1987 issue of *National Geographic* called "The Prodigious Soybean." Twenty-five pages long, it's a glowing testimonial to this most glorious and versatile of foods. The photography is exquisite, and the article is well researched and easy to read. The soybean, by the way, has been used as a staple in the Asian diet for more than 3,000 years.

TIPS & SHORTCUTS

Alert! Tofu does not melt. When you see any product labeled soy cheese, read the ingredients on the label. If you see the ingredient *casein*, you may want to consider putting the package back on the shelf. Gluey in texture, casein is an element in milk, and also the key ingredient in high-quality carpenter's wood glue. It gives that extra stickiness that woodworkers need. Manufacturers who put casein in tofu and call it soy cheese may not be all that concerned about your health. Be aware, choose consciously, and read labels.

❖ When you mix tofu in the blender, don't put in a whole block at once. Instead, crumble it a little bit at a time. It mixes much easier this way.

❖ When you store tofu in the refrigerator, cover it, store it in purified water, and change the water each day. This takes only minutes.

❖ One cup tofu equals $1/2$ pound.

❖ Should you decide to sauté tofu cubes to include with your stir-fry dishes, you might want to dredge them in a mix of $1/2$ cup flour and $1/4$ cup nutritional yeast first—a dramatic flavor enhancement.

❖ How to freeze tofu: Cut firm or extra-firm tofu (not silken) into 2" x 2" slabs about $1/2$" thick, blotting them well. Place them in a plastic container in single layers. Place wax paper between the layers. Don't add water. Cover with a lid. Freeze for about 6–8 hours. I use frozen tofu within two weeks, simply because almost all frozen foods begin to devitalize after that length of time.

❖ Thaw frozen tofu by pouring boiling water over it, then squeeze it well. It thaws immediately.

❖ Blot tofu by wrapping it in a clean cloth and squeezing it gently to remove excess moisture.

TOFU NO-MEAT BALLS, SEE PAGE 57

Quick & Easy Stir-Fry Combinations

With all these combos, sauté in one tablespoon sesame oil for about 8–10 minutes. So quick, so easy, so delicious.

Combo #1

8 stalks asparagus, sliced julienne in 2" pieces

4 cloves garlic, sliced (or 1 teaspoon garlic powder or flakes)

6 mushrooms, washed and sliced

1/2 head fresh cabbage, thinly sliced

1/2 to 1 pound tofu, cut in 1/2" x 3" x 3" slices

Sprinkle with tamari and serve over steaming hot rice

Combo #2

3 cups cooked, diced potatoes

1 golden onion, thinly sliced

2 cloves chopped garlic or 1 teaspoon garlic powder

1/2 teaspoon black pepper, freshly ground

1 cup green beans, sliced julienne in 2" pieces

1/2 cup black olives

Sprinkle with tamari and serve with a mixed green salad

Combo #3

3 cups zucchini, sliced julienne in 1/4" pieces

2 cloves garlic, minced (or 1 teaspoon garlic powder)

6 large mushrooms, sliced

2 large tomatoes, chopped

1/4 cup shredded carrots

Sprinkle with tamari and serve over hot couscous or pasta

Combo #4

3 cups broccoli florets, peeled and sliced, with leaves

2 cloves garlic, minced (or 1 teaspoon garlic powder)

2 cups potatoes, cooked and diced

2 cups cooked acorn or other yellow squash

Sprinkle with tamari and serve in pita pockets

Combo #5

2 cups cabbage, finely shredded

1/2 cup carrots, finely shredded

1/2 cup broccoli florets, peeled and sliced

1/2 cup firm tofu, cubed (1/2")

Stir in:

1/4 cup hoisin sauce (available in the Asian foods section of your supermarket)

A self-contained meal!

Top any of these Quick Stir-Fry dishes with your choice of: sesame seeds, sunflower seeds, almond slices, pignolas (pine nuts), chopped walnuts, ground peanuts, black olives, or crushed garlic croutons.

If you want to add an Asian flavor to Quick Stir-Fry dishes, use the 3-minutes-to-prepare **Quick & Easy No-Cook Teriyaki Sauce** (see pg. 120).

TOFU NO-MEAT BALLS

You will fool just about anyone who must have meat with their spaghetti. Quick, easy, and very tasty.

- **PREPARATION TIME: 10 minutes**
- **COOKING TIME: 10–15 minutes**
- **YIELD: 24 non-meat balls**

1 pound firm tofu, drained, blotted, and mashed
1/2 cup uncooked rolled oats
2 Tablespoons tamari
1/4 cup parsley, minced
2 teaspoons onion powder
1 teaspoon garlic powder

Combine all ingredients in medium-size mixing bowl and use your hands to mix well. Shape into 1 1/2" balls, and roll in a mixture of:

1 cup whole-wheat pastry flour
1/2 cup nutritional yeast

Sauté in a little sesame oil until uniformly browned. Add to your favorite marinara sauce-based dish. Voilà!

See picture, page 55

TOFU-CHILADAS

Tofu-chiladas go especially well with **Mexican Rice** *(see pg. 44) and* **Sara's Mexican Salad** *(see pg. 104). This recipe is a favorite meal for growing teens—not only to eat, but also to prepare. You'll be asked for this recipe again and again. It's a real winner.*

The night before, freeze tofu.
- **PREPARATION TIME: 30 minutes**
- **BAKING TIME: 20–25 minutes**
- **SERVES: 4 teenage boys or 6 adults**

2 pounds frozen tofu

1/4 cup tamari

One 6-ounce can tomato paste

2 teaspoons onion powder

1 teaspoon cumin, ground

1 teaspoon garlic powder

3 Tablespoons chili powder

One 28-ounce can peeled whole Roma tomatoes

1 Tablespoon extra virgin olive oil

2 12-ounce cans black olives, drained and sliced

3 medium ripe avocados

4 cups enchilada sauce

12 sprouted-wheat or whole-wheat tortillas

Preheat oven to 350°. Thaw frozen tofu by pouring boiling water over it. Squeeze it well. Combine in bowl: tamari, tomato paste, onion powder, cumin, garlic powder, and chili powder. Stir briskly with a fork until well mixed. Crumble the squeezed tofu into the mix, coating it well. Sauté mixture briskly in oil until slightly browned. Add tomatoes, breaking them apart with your hands. Sauté a few moments longer until heated through.

Cut avocados lengthwise, and slice each half into six 1/4" slices. Place enchilada sauce in a bowl, and dip each tortilla in it. Then place tortilla on plate, putting 1/2 cup filling down the center. On top of the filling, place several avocado slices and about a tablespoon of olives. Roll up the tofu-chilada and place flap-side down in a glass baking dish. Do this for each enchilada until all ingredients are used. Cover with any remaining sauce and top generously with olive slices. Bake for 20–25 minutes until hot and bubbly.

∽

I will never forget the first time I served this dish. My son Luke had his friend Mark over for dinner one evening. Mark, being accustomed to having meat inside his tortillas, looked at his dinner, then glanced sideways at Luke, not wanting to question out loud and appear impolite, but questioning nonetheless. Luke, known for his acerbic wit, said casually, "Don't worry, Mark. Nothing on your plate ever had a mother."

See picture on next page

Tofu-chiladas

Burgers

Without burgers, this book would not be complete. They can be a lot of fun to create, even more fun to assemble, and a dazzling treat to bite into. Oats, rice, tofu—select your favorite and create a burger you won't believe. You can fry, broil, bake, or barbecue any of these burgers; let the occasion dictate the method of cooking!

When my children's friends came for dinner, the burgers they were served were very different from those they were accustomed to having at home or at a fast-food restaurant. They knew they weren't getting meat, but they were never quite sure exactly what was inside that bun. When I was training to become a paralegal, studying the intricacies of probate law, I heard a phrase that tickled me because of the double entendre. The kids thought it was funny, too, so I made it into a small sign and put it on the dining room wall. It said simply, "Beware of ambiguities in your codicils."

A few days later, my daughter Sara had her friend Sylvia to dinner, and we had burgers. Right after we said grace, Sylvia spotted the sign. She looked down at her plate cautiously, then glanced slowly around the table, trying to be as casual as possible, waiting for someone else to take that first bite. In a flash, we got what had happened, and we all started to laugh. Once we explained the sign, she laughed louder than the rest of us! The sign came down.

EARTH BURGER

This is sumptuous as a burger-in-a-bun and can also double as a main dish served with a baked potato topped with avocado slices or **No-Oil Tahini Dressing** *(see pg. 113). Mmm-mm good!*

- **PREPARATION TIME: 10 minutes**
- **YIELD: 6 burgers**

1 small onion
2 cloves garlic
1 teaspoon sesame oil
3 cups cooked rice
1 cup walnuts, finely ground
2 Tablespoons tahini
1/4 cup carrots, grated
1/4 cup fresh parsley, finely chopped
2 Tablespoons tomato juice
1/2 cup yellow cornmeal
3 Tablespoons nutritional yeast

Sauté onion and garlic in oil. Quickly blend all ingredients except cornmeal and nutritional yeast in a food processor. Shape the mix into patties. Mix cornmeal and nutritional yeast together, then gently dust each patty with the mixture before cooking. Sauté, barbecue, or bake at 375°, 20–25 minutes.

See picture, page 62

OAT BURGER

Delicious as a burger-in-a-bun, and also as a main dish with potatoes, mushroom gravy, and a crisp mixed-greens salad.

- **PREPARATION TIME: 10 minutes**
- **COOKING TIME: 5 minutes**
- **YIELD: 6 burgers**

3 Tablespoons tamari*
4 cups water*
2 1/2 cups raw rolled oats*
1 medium onion, minced
1/2 cup fresh parsley, finely chopped
3 Tablespoons nutritional yeast
1 teaspoon garlic powder
1/2 teaspoon sea salt
1 Tablespoon tahini
3/4 cup walnuts, finely ground
Pinch ground oregano
1/2 teaspoon dried basil

*Or use cooked oatmeal, stirring in tamari.

Heat water and tamari to boiling, then turn down heat and add oats. Cook 5 minutes and cool. Mix remaining ingredients in blender. When oats are cool, mix all ingredients together. Form into patties. Bake, sauté, or barbecue. These are especially wonderful when baked.

EARTH BURGERS, SEE PAGE 61

SERVING SUGGESTIONS

There's an infinite variety of ways to serve burgers! One of the most exciting parts of creating veggie-burgers is giving them their final form. You can have them reflect almost any part of the world or palate with these final touches. First, create the burger patty of your choice, then add the trimmings. Experiment! Here are a few combinations I've found most popular among my family and friends. Invent your own favorites!

FRENCH BARBECUE
Sliced French roll spread with **Ghee** (see pg. 40) or butter
Barbecue sauce

ONION SLICES
Use thin onion slices that have been gently sautéed or burned. "Burned" usually means "mistake," but when onions are blackened and still soft, they're quite good. My friend, Sark, wouldn't have them any other way! Serve with Greek peperoncini.

ALOHA HAWAIIAN
Whole-grain bun
Tofu Mayonnaise (see pg. 122)
Layers of lettuce
2–3 thin tomato slices
2 thin dill pickle slices
1 fresh pineapple slice sautéed in tamari
Quick & Easy No-Cook Teriyaki Sauce (see pg. 120)

Arrange all the above on the bun, leaving the burger for last. Dip the hot, cooked burger into the warm no-cook teriyaki sauce and place on bun, pouring more teriyaki sauce on top of burger. Top with bun. This burger is a real hit with sweet & sour fans. Be sure you have extra napkins on hand. It's juicy!

SILLY VALLEY
In honor of its name, we always serve this burger with chips.

Sprouted-wheat bun
Tofu mayonnaise on one half
Dijon mustard on one half
4–5 very thin tomato slices
4–5 avocado slices that have been sprinkled with Spike®
Combination of greens: escarole, raddichio, watercress, romaine, butter lettuce, red lettuce
Combination of sprouts: sunflower, buckwheat, and alfalfa
2–3 thin dill pickle slices
Sprinkle raw sunflower seeds over all

TO BAKE BURGERS
Dip uncooked burger in breading mix, place on lightly oiled non-aluminum baking pan, and bake at 375°, 20–25 minutes. Turn once to brown evenly on both sides.

BREADING MIX
Mix together in a bowl:
1/4 cup whole-wheat pastry flour
1/4 cup nutritional yeast
1/2 cup cornmeal
1/4 teaspoon sea salt

TO SAUTÉ BURGERS
In a heavy skillet—preferably but not necessarily
cast iron—sauté burgers over medium heat in a little
sesame oil until golden brown, turning once or twice
to brown evenly. Blot on a brown paper bag to absorb
any excess oil.

TO BARBECUE BURGERS
Cook burgers on a grill, as you would barbecue
anything else. Vegetable burgers taste especially
magnificent when they're basted with marinade or
barbecue sauce as they're cooking.

TO BROIL BURGERS
Place on non-aluminum baking sheet and broil on
each side about 5–8 minutes. Keep an eye on them to
make sure they're cooked to the exact doneness you
prefer.

LEFTOVER BURGER PATTIES
Make extras and freeze for later.

AS EASY AS SOUP

"To know the way and not to practice it is to be a soup ladle in the pot,
and not taste the flavor of the soup."

— FROM *BUDDHA'S LITTLE INSTRUCTION BOOK,* BY JACK KORNFIELD

Soup

TIPS & SHORTCUTS

Anyone can make a delectable soup. The secrets are in a tasty, rich broth base and just the right herbs and seasonings. This chapter shows you the basic steps and opens up possibilities for you to create your own. My daughter Sara started creating her own favorite soup combinations at about the age of eight or nine. Some were pretty wild, but through trial and error, she learned what tasted good and what just didn't work. Kids aren't limited when it comes to mixing herbs, vegetables, and grains. Just turn them loose and let them experiment!

THE BASIC STOCK & VARIATIONS

Basic Stock
Make it a habit to save the parts of raw vegetables that are usually discarded: carrot ends; celery root ends; and the outer leaves of lettuce, kale, cabbage, etc. Wash them well and keep them in a container in the freezer. They're a gold mine of valuable minerals and flavor.

When you're ready to make your broth, take the vegetable parts from the freezer and place them in a 6- to 8-quart pot, covering them with four times as much water as there are scraps. Bring to a boil, then simmer for about 40 minutes until the broth is a rich golden color. Strain and save broth. Discard vegetables. Keep broth tightly covered in refrigerator. Use within three days, or freeze for later. This broth is also excellent for instant use in gravies and stews.

When you boil vegetables, save the water they're boiled in. "Yam broth" makes one of the most delicious gravies or soups you've ever tasted.

If you've run out of Basic Stock and need some in a hurry, dissolve four vegetable bouillon cubes in one quart of boiling water.

VARIATIONS

Basic Brown Broth

COMBINE:
2 quarts Basic Stock
1/4 cup nutritional yeast
1/4 cup tamari
1/4 teaspoon garlic powder
1 teaspoon dried basil

Zingy Gazpacho, see page 68

Basic Tomato Broth

COMBINE:
2 quarts Basic Stock
1/4 cup tamari
1/4 cup nutritional yeast
One 8-ounce can tomato sauce
2 teaspoons dried basil
1/4 teaspoon black pepper
Pinch cinnamon

Basic Broth-in-A-Hurry

DISSOLVE:
4 vegetable bouillon cubes in
   2 quarts boiling water

TO THICKEN SOUP

10 MINUTES BEFORE SERVING SOUP, COMBINE
IN A LIDDED JAR:
1/4 cup flour (potato flour is best, but whole-wheat
   pastry flour works fine)
1 cup cold water

Put cap on jar and shake vigorously until mixture is smooth and creamy with no raw flour left, and no lumps. Add to soup, stirring continuously. Broth thickens within minutes.

ZINGY GAZPACHO

*This soup is lovely by itself, yet a natural with **Sara's Mexican Salad** (see pg. 104) or **Tofu-chiladas** (see pg. 58).*

• **PREPARATION TIME: 10 minutes**
• **CHILL FOR: 1 hour**
• **SERVES: 6**

3 cups tomato juice
3 fresh Roma tomatoes, peeled and diced
1 cucumber, diced
1 bell pepper, 1/2 grated, 1/2 minced
1 Tablespoon parsley, minced fresh
1 Tablespoon apple cider vinegar
Juice of 1/2 lemon
1 clove garlic, finely minced
Sea salt to taste

Mix well. Chill one hour before serving.

See picture, page 67

Sara's Minestrone: Soup-for-a-Group!

This recipe is my daughter Sara's variation of an old family favorite. It's a natural with garlic bread. (It's easy to reduce the amount of ingredients for fewer persons.)

• **PREPARATION TIME: 15 minutes (with food processor)**
• **COOKING TIME: 30 minutes**
• **SERVES: 10**

4 quarts **Basic Broth** (brown or tomato) (see pg. 66 & 68)
1/2 cup dry (or one 15-ounce can) kidney beans
One 28-ounce can whole tomatoes, peeled, with liquid
1/2 cup string beans, cut (1/2")
1/2 cup zucchini, cubed (1/2")
1 medium carrot, diced
1 cup fresh or frozen peas
2 ribs celery, diced
1 small golden onion, minced
4 cloves garlic, minced
2 cups cabbage, shredded
1 medium red potato, cubed (about 1 cup)
1/4 cup parsley, chopped
Fresh corn scraped from 3 cobs
1 green bell pepper, diced
One 8-ounce can garbanzo beans
One 8-ounce can kidney beans
1 cup mushrooms, thinly sliced and quartered
1 bay leaf
1/2 teaspoon ground oregano, or 2 Tablespoons fresh, chopped
1/2 teaspoon dried thyme, or 2 Tablespoons fresh, chopped

1 teaspoon dried basil, or 1/4 cup fresh, chopped
1/4 teaspoon black pepper, coarsely ground
Sea salt to taste
1 cup broken vermicelli pasta

A food processor really saves time with this recipe. Heat broth to boiling, and add all ingredients except vermicelli. Simmer together 30 minutes. Five minutes before serving, break vermicelli into 3" pieces and add to soup. Cook about 5 minutes, then thicken soup (see Tips & Shortcuts for "how to"). Simmer 5 more minutes, stirring, until somewhat thickened. What a soup!

❧

We used to have a family tradition that caused the kids to poke carefully around in their soup when it was first served: Whoever had the bay leaf in their bowl did that evening's dishes. Although they're adults now, whenever they eat minestrone, they still peer at their soup cautiously and casually stir the spoon around before they take that first bite!

BROCCOLI & BARLEY SOUP

This robust soup is ideally suited for a cold winter's night, served with your favorite hearty bread.

- **PREPARATION TIME: 10 minutes**
- **COOKING TIME: 20 minutes**
- **SERVES: 6**

6 cups **Basic Brown Broth** (see pg. 66)
1/4 cup Dr. Bronner's Bouillon (or tamari)
1/4 cup nutritional yeast
1/2 teaspoon onion powder
1/2 teaspoon garlic powder
2 cups broccoli, peeled and coarsely chopped
1 cup barley
1 carrot, diced
Sea salt to taste
2 teaspoons dill weed
1/4 teaspoon cayenne
2 cloves garlic, sliced lengthwise

Bring broth almost to a boil. Add remaining ingredients and simmer over medium heat 20 minutes. Just before you're ready to serve, thicken broth. (See beginning of this section for "how to.") That's all there is to it! Couldn't be easier, couldn't be tastier.

ASPARAGUS SOUP

The unusual flavor of this springtime soup becomes dramatic when served with hot French bread. To add the gourmet touch, have a bowl of warmed, garlic-flavored extra virgin olive oil handy to dip the bread in. Oh, my!

- **PREPARATION TIME: 10 minutes**
- **COOKING TIME: 10 minutes**
- **SERVES: 4**

8 scallions, chopped (including healthy green tops)
2 Tablespoons **Ghee** (see pg. 40) or butter
3 red potatoes (with skins), chopped
3 veggie bouillon cubes, dissolved in
   4 cups hot water
2 pounds fresh asparagus
4 ribs celery, chopped
1/4 teaspoon ground nutmeg
1/2 teaspoon salt (or to taste)
1/4 teaspoon freshly ground black pepper

Snap off cut end of asparagus stalks and discard. Sauté scallions in ghee or butter until soft. Put all ingredients in large pot and cook over medium heat until tender, about 10–15 minutes. Purée at least 3/4 of the soup in blender, then add to the original mixture, stirring well. Yum!

See picture on next page

ASPARAGUS SOUP

BLACK BEAN SOUP

This soup is especially outrageous served with steaming hot rice.

Soak dry beans the night before, or use canned.
- **PREPARATION TIME: 15 minutes**
- **COOKING TIME: 3 hours (15 minutes with canned beans)**
- **SERVES: 6**

1 1/2 cups dried black beans (or one 15-ounce can)
2 quarts **Basic Brown Broth** (see pg. 66)
1 small onion, minced
2 carrots, diced
1 rib celery, minced
1/4 cup bell pepper, diced
1 bay leaf, broken in half
Juice of 1 small lemon
1/2 teaspoon dry mustard
1 teaspoon sea salt
1/4 teaspoon black pepper, coarsely ground
1 teaspoon apple cider vinegar
1/4 teaspoon nutmeg
1/2 teaspoon coriander
1/2 teaspoon peeled and grated gingerroot
Tamari to taste

Wash and pick through dry beans, then soak overnight. The next day, drain and discard the water. Place beans in large non-aluminum pot, and cover with Basic Broth, to about 2" above beans. Bring to a boil, then reduce to a simmer. Cover and cook 2 1/2 hours or until beans are tender. Add rest of ingredients and cook an additional 20 minutes. Add water, if needed, as the beans are cooking. If you're using canned beans, cook 15 minutes with other ingredients.

VEGETABLES

"The act of putting into your mouth what the earth has grown is perhaps your most direct interaction with the earth."

— FROM *DIET FOR A SMALL PLANET,* BY FRANCES MOORE LAPPE

MEXICAN YAMS, SEE PAGE 82

List of Vegetables

Here is a basic list of vegetables to consider when you do your grocery shopping.

- ✤ Artichoke
- ✤ Asparagus
- ✤ Avocado
- ✤ Beans
  - • Lima
  - • String
- ✤ Broccoli
- ✤ Cabbage
  - • Green
  - • Red
- ✤ Carrot
- ✤ Cauliflower
- ✤ Celery
- ✤ Corn
- ✤ Cucumber
- ✤ Eggplant
- ✤ Escarole
- ✤ Leeks
- ✤ Lettuce
  - • Bibb
- • Green leaf
- • Raddichio
- • Red leaf
- • Romaine
- ✤ Onion
  - • Bermuda
  - • White
  - • Yellow
- ✤ Parsnip
- ✤ Peas
  - • Chinese sugar (edible pod)
- ✤ Potato
  - • Red (Irish)
  - • Russet (baking)
- ✤ Pumpkin
- ✤ Radish
- ✤ Scallion
- ✤ Spinach
- ✤ Squash, summer (soft skin)
  - • Crookneck
  - • Fluted summer Zucchini
- ✤ Squash, winter (hard rind)
  - • Acorn
  - • Banana
  - • Butternut
  - • Kabocha
  - • Spaghetti
- ✤ Sweet Potato
- ✤ Tomato
- ✤ Turnip
- ✤ Yam

TIPS & SHORTCUTS

- ❖ The highest mineral content of vegetables lies just under the skin. This is lost when they're peeled, so avoid peeling whenever possible.

- ❖ Save the water you've cooked your vegetables in and use it for soup stock or gravy; it's high in precious minerals.

- ❖ Eating vegetables and raw fruits at the same meal can cause intestinal gas.

- ❖ A subtle touch for sautéeing vegetables is to add just a few shakes of tamari as they're sizzling in the pan, only seconds away from being served. Then sprinkle lightly with a few shakes of nutritional yeast, stir quickly and serve.

- ❖ Another way to tease out the flavor is to take about a cup of crisp garlic croutons, crush them, and distribute them over any stir-fry or sautéed vegetable.

MIX & MATCH VEGGIES

A meal in itself, this is quick & easy to serve over a steaming hot grain such as rice, couscous, quinoa, or millet. A super quick dinner that is fabulous and filling!

- **PREPARATION TIME: 10 minutes**
- **COOKING TIME: 15 minutes**
- **SERVES: 6**

2 bunches broccoli, peeled and sliced
2 golden onions, thinly sliced
1 red bell pepper, thinly sliced
1 green bell pepper, thinly sliced
2 cups bean sprouts
1 Tablespoon sesame oil
6 large mushrooms, sliced
4 large tomatoes, chopped
1 12-ounce can pitted black olives, drained
2 Tablespoons nutritional yeast
1 Tablespoon tamari

Steam broccoli for 5–8 minutes. Sauté onions 3 minutes in oil. Add all the vegetables, olives, yeast, and tamari, and stir, heating through. Serve over your favorite cooked grain.

POTATOES BOMBAY

This quick-to-make Indian dish is delightful served with a side touch of Indian chutney as a condiment. Add your favorite green steamed vegetable and you have a gourmet feast!

- **PREPARATION TIME: 15 minutes**
- **COOKING TIME: 7 minutes**
- **SERVES: 4**

1 package frozen (or 2 cups fresh) peas
3 Tablespoons sesame oil
3 Tablespoons curry powder (see pg. 122)
4 cups unpeeled cooked potatoes, diced
One 16-ounce can whole peeled tomatoes, drained
1/4 cup parsley, chopped
Pinch crushed red pepper flakes

Cook peas and drain, saving liquid for soup broth. Heat skillet over medium heat and add oil. Quickly stir in curry powder and add peas, then potatoes, stirring briskly the whole time. Add tomatoes, parsley, and pepper flakes, heating through. Serve immediately.

SPAGHETTI SQUASH
(SUPER LOW-CAL)

Your friends and family will rave about this one! Low-fat, delicious, and gently filling. Serve with a simple green salad tossed with **No-Oil Tahini Dressing** *(see pg. 113) and French bread.*

- **PREPARATION TIME: 5 minutes**
- **BAKING TIME: 45 minutes**
- **YIELD: Depends on size of squash**

1 spaghetti squash (select size of squash to fit your needs)
1 recipe **Basic Marinara Sauce** (see pg.49)

Preheat oven to 400°. Here's where your vegetable cleaver comes in handy. Place squash on cutting board and use cleaver to slice squash in half lengthwise. Scoop out seeds and strings and discard them. Place squash cut-side down in non-aluminum baking dish. Add 1" of water and bake 45 minutes.

While squash is baking, prepare Basic Marinara Sauce. When squash is done, scoop out the spaghetti-like strands and serve, topping with sauce as though it were spaghetti. Incredible!

BAKED ACORN SQUASH

Serve with rice and steamed broccoli or brussels sprouts. Quick, easy, and sooooo flavorful. Oh my! Will you ever get startled "Ooh's" and "Aah's" for this one! Who ever thought squash could taste this good?!

- **PREPARATION TIME: 10 minutes**
- **BAKING TIME: 1 hour**
- **SERVES: 4**

2 acorn squash
1/4 cup **Ghee** (see pg. 40) or butter, melted
2 teaspoons cinnamon
1/2 teaspoon nutmeg
1/2 teaspoon fresh gingerroot, peeled and grated
1 teaspoon sea salt
1/2 cup honey or barley malt syrup

Use vegetable cleaver to cut squash in half length-wise. Scoop out and discard seeds and strings. Place cut-side down in glass or ceramic baking dish and add 1" of water. Bake uncovered for 40 minutes. Meanwhile, combine other ingredients in a small covered jar, shaking them together to mix well. A rubber spatula helps mix in the sweetener. After the squash have baked for 30 minutes, turn them over, cut-side up, pierce the "flesh" a few times, and pour mixture into the squash cavities. Bake an additional 15 minutes.

See picture, page 19

SHEPHERD'S PIE

This is an easy meal to prepare, yet your guests will think you spent hours in the kitchen. Great on a chilly evening. A simple green salad is a lovely accompaniment.

- **PREPARATION TIME: 20 minutes**
- **BAKING TIME: 40 minutes**
- **YIELD: 6 servings**

4 russet (baking) potatoes
3 Tablespoons **Ghee** (see pg. 40) or butter
1/2 teaspoon onion powder
1/2 teaspoon black pepper, coarsely ground
2 cups **Basic Gravy** (see pg. 117)
1 medium golden onion, sliced
1/2 cup green beans, julienne sliced
1/2 cup zucchini or crookneck squash, diced
1 large carrot, julienne sliced
1 large parsnip, diced
1/2 cup peas, fresh or frozen
1 cup mushrooms, sliced

Preheat oven to 375°. Scrub and cube (but do not peel) potatoes. Cook in boiling water 20 minutes or until tender. Drain and mash, adding ghee, onion powder, and pepper. Set aside. Steam remaining vegetables for 5 minutes. Place them in a 3-quart casserole dish and cover with gravy, mixing well. Cover with mashed potatoes and bake at 375° for 40 minutes until golden brown.

See picture on next page

SHEPHERD'S PIE

VEGGIE WRAP COMBINATIONS

Any of these suggested veggie wraps go well with a large green salad. Quick, easy, and delicious, you won't believe how quickly they get to the table—and how quickly they disappear!

- **PREPARATION TIME: 10 minutes**
- **COOKING TIME: 15 minutes**
- **SERVES: 6**

VEGGIE COMBO

1 medium head of broccoli
2 Tablespoons tamari
2 Tablespoons water
1 1/2 cups mushrooms, sliced
1/2 red bell pepper, chopped
2 medium zucchini, sliced
1 medium golden onion, chopped
2 red potatoes, diced
One 12-ounce can pitted black olives, drained
1/3 cup nutritional yeast
6 sprouted-wheat or whole-wheat tortillas

Preheat oven to 350°. Separate broccoli florets, then peel and slice stems in 1/8" thick rounds. Slice the florets as you would a mushroom. Heat heavy skillet and add tamari and water. Add all vegetables and olives, and sauté for about 10 minutes. Sprinkle mixture with nutritional yeast, and gently mix it in.

Sauté another 5 minutes. Heat tortillas in a dry skillet. Place on serving plate and fill with vegetable mixture. Roll up, securing with a toothpick, if necessary. Serve flap-side down.

SWEET & SOUR COMBO

Goes well with hot Udon noodles. Drizzle with more **Chinese Sweet & Sour Sauce** *(see pg. 120). Fabulous!*

- **FILLING PREPARATION TIME: 15 minutes**
- **SWEET & SOUR SAUCE PREPARATION TIME: 5 minutes**

6 sprouted-wheat or whole-wheat tortillas
1/4 cup water
2 Tablespoons tamari
2 cups broccoli, peeled and sliced, broken into small florets
6 mushrooms, sliced
1 bunch green onions, chopped, including healthy greens

In skillet, stir-fry broccoli with water and tamari for 5 minutes. Add mushrooms and onions, stirring everything together for two minutes. (Save any water that's left, and freeze for soup broth.) Place tortillas, one at a time, in dry skillet, and warm over medium heat. Remove from skillet. Place 1/6 of filling down middle of each tortilla. Pour 2 Tablespoons **Sweet & Sour Sauce** over filling, and roll up tortilla, then place flap-side down on dinner plate.

Mexicana Combo

*Goes well with **Sara's Mexican Salad** (see pg. 104), or with steaming hot basmati rice. A favorite of weight- and taste-conscious people of all ages! This is incredibly good.*

- **PREPARATION TIME: 15 minutes**
- **COOKING TIME: 15 minutes** • **SERVES: 6**

1 onion, chopped

2 cloves garlic, minced

4 Roma tomatoes, chopped

$1/4$ cup green bell pepper, chopped

1 cup tomato sauce

$1/2$ teaspoon apple cider vinegar

1 Tablespoon chili powder

$1^1/2$ teaspoons sea salt

$1/2$ cup sliced black olives

6 sprouted-wheat or whole-wheat tortillas

Place all ingredients (except tortillas) in a skillet, bring to slow boil, then reduce heat and cover pan. Simmer on low heat for 15 minutes.

Preheat oven to 325°. Prepare each tortilla: Place tortilla in dry skillet over medium heat to warm. Fill flat tortilla with $1/6$ of the filling, then wrap it up as you would a burrito, placing flap-side down in a ceramic or glass baking pan. Keep finished tortillas in warm oven until all of them are ready.

Even More Combinations . . .

Try any of these, using the same directions for preparation. Consider them guidelines only, with the goal being the creation of your own delicious mixtures!

Variation #1

2 cups string beans, julienne sliced in $1/2$" pieces

8 scallions, including healthy green tops

3 cloves garlic, minced

1 teaspoon fresh gingerroot, peeled and grated

Variation #2

2 cups whole Chinese snow peas

1 bunch scallions

6 mushrooms, sliced

1 clove garlic, minced

Variation #3

2 cups cubed (1") eggplant

1 cup green or red bell pepper, sliced thin

$1/2$ cup celery chopped

2 cloves garlic

See picture, page ii

ARTICHOKES

*A great accompaniment for artichokes are baked potatoes topped with avocado slices. You may be accustomed to dipping the leaves in mayonnaise or **Ghee** (see pg. 40). Just for the fun of it, experiment by not dipping them in anything; just savor their unique flavor all by itself.*

- **PREPARATION TIME: 10 minutes**
- **COOKING TIME: 45 minutes**
- **SERVES: 4**

4 medium artichokes
2 cloves garlic
1/2 teaspoon extra virgin olive oil

With kitchen shears, snip off thorny tips of artichoke leaves and discard. Trim off just the dried bottom of the stem. Gently pull open artichoke leaves slightly, and run cold water through them to rinse thoroughly. Put 2" of water in large saucepan, and add garlic and oil. Place artichokes in water, stem side down, and bring water to a boil. Cover, and simmer for 45 minutes or until outer leaves pull off easily. Cooking time is reduced by cutting artichoke in half lengthwise before cooking.

See picture on next page

MEXICAN YAMS

A gentle complement to basmati rice and steamed broccoli.

- **PREPARATION TIME: 10 minutes**
- **COOKING TIME: 10 minutes**
- **SERVES: 3**

2 Tablespoons sesame oil
2 cups yams (Red Garnets if available), sliced in 1/4" rounds
1/2 cup green bell pepper, sliced julienne
1/2 cup golden onions, sliced thin
Sea salt to taste
1 teaspoon cumin
1/2 teaspoon chili powder
Tamari

Sauté all ingredients together in a skillet until yams are cooked through and peppers and onions are soft. Sprinkle lightly with tamari.

See picture, page 74

ARTICHOKES

BELL PEPPER EXTRAVAGANZA

This dish goes well with your favorite pasta or basmati rice. The colors of the peppers are especially dramatic over the white rice. Perfect with a simple green salad tossed with oil and vinegar dressing.

The fun of this dish is to combine green, red, purple-black, orange, and yellow bell peppers not only for flavor, but for vibrant color as well. Use a large skillet. The peppers reduce in size as you sauté them, so a 12" skillet will work well.

- **PREPARATION TIME: 15 minutes**
- **COOKING TIME: 10 minutes**
- **SERVES: 4–6**

1/4 cup extra virgin olive oil
8 medium (about 8 cups) bell peppers of all colors
6 medium garlic cloves, minced
1/2 cup fresh parsley, chopped
3 Tablespoons lemon juice
1 1/2 teaspoons salt
1/4 teaspoon black pepper, coarsely ground

Cut peppers in half, remove stems and seeds, and cut into 1/4" strips. Heat oil over medium heat, add peppers, and sauté about 10 minutes, or until tender. Add garlic and sauté 30 seconds, then stir in parsley, lemon juice, and black pepper. That's it!

❧

My daughter Jean-Marie was the one I took with me when I went shopping for this dish. When we came to the greengrocer's bell pepper section, I just looked at her, smiled, and said, "Choose your favorite colors; I'll tell you when to stop." I held open a large bag for her. She picked up each pepper, turned it over in her hand, looked at it this way and that, and chose the winners with great deliberation and care before she dropped them into the bag. Once she had filled it with red, yellow, green, orange, and purple treasures, her demeanor was like that of a queen who had made some very important decisions.

See picture, page 6

VEGGIES EASTERN STYLE

Quick & easy, and yummy, too, this dish goes well with rice, millet, or couscous. Chutney is the ideal condiment.

- **PREPARATION TIME: 5 minutes**
- **COOKING TIME: 10 minutes**
- **SERVES: 4**

2 Tablespoons tamari
2 Tablespoons water
2 medium onions, chopped
3 cups cauliflower, broken into florets and sliced
3 cups broccoli, peeled, broken into florets and sliced
2 teaspoons curry powder (see pg. 122)
1/4 cup dry roasted peanuts, coarsely chopped
1/4 cup raisins

Place vegetables in a skillet with tamari and water, and sprinkle curry powder over them. Cover and gently steam for about 10 minutes. Add nuts and raisins.

If you have teenagers, you may want to double this recipe. For some reason, they devour this as though it were going out of style.

SIOBHAN'S GREEK BEANS

The taste of these beans is most extraordinary. They are delicious over rice or pasta, or served simply with French bread and a bowl of garlic-flavored extra virgin olive oil to dip it in. A mixed-greens salad with oil-vinegar dressing is the perfect complement.

- **PREPARATION TIME: 10 minutes**
- **COOKING TIME: 20–30 minutes**
- **SERVES: 6**

2 pounds fresh string beans
1/4 cup extra virgin olive oil
1 large yellow onion, sliced
3 cloves garlic, sliced
One 28-ounce can skinless tomatoes, diced or crushed
1 bunch fresh parsley, chopped
Salt to taste
A few twists of black pepper, freshly ground

Cut off and discard ends of beans, and remove strings. Cut beans into 1 1/2" pieces. Put oil in a 2-quart saucepan and sauté onion and garlic. Add beans and tomatoes to onion-garlic mixture, season with salt and pepper, bring to a boil, then simmer uncovered for about 20–30 minutes.

See picture, page x

PURÉE MEDLEY

Purées add the finishing touch. There's nothing quite like a simple, tasty vegetable side dish used as an accompaniment to a grain, legume, tofu, or other-vegetable-based entrée. The enhanced flavor will make you say, "It's so easy! Why didn't I think of this?" Purées served over baked potatoes, asparagus, broccoli, brussels' sprouts, parsnips, you name it—will cause your reputation as a cook to go up notches! Purées take only minutes to prepare, and their versatility is endless. I'm presenting only a few examples here, and I invite you to experiment with your own favorite vegetable-herb combinations. Whatever vegetables you have too much of in your refrigerator is fair game. Stretch your imagination and expand your repertoire!

Any one of these medley variations takes 5 minutes to prepare, 10–12 minutes to cook, and yields about 4 cups.

. . . WITH CARROTS

1 vegetable bouillon cube dissolved in
  $1/2$ cup boiling water
10 carrots, chopped
2 Tablespoons non-alcoholic Rouge wine
1 teaspoon tamari
$1/4$ teaspoon cumin
$1/4$ teaspoon nutmeg
1 Tablespoon unsweetened coconut, finely shredded

Chop carrots. Dissolve bouillon cube in boiling water. Cook carrots in this broth until they're slightly soft. Pour off broth and set aside. (Freeze for your next soup or bean/grain dish.) Put all other ingredients into blender and spin to a purée consistency.

PURÉE MEDLEY WITH YAMS, SEE PAGE 88

. . . WITH BEETS

4 medium to large fresh beets, cut in half (about 4 cups)
3 cloves garlic, chopped
2 Tablespoons non-alcoholic Rouge wine
Pinch cinnamon
Sea salt to taste

Cook beets in enough water to barely cover them. Cooking time depends on size of beets; usually it takes about 10-15 minutes. When the beets can be pierced easily, they're done. Remove from heat and cool slightly. Slip off beet skins and discard them. Place beets with remaining ingredients in blender, and spin until of purée consistency.

. . . WITH YAMS

2–3 medium fresh yams (about 4 cups). The deep orange-fleshed Red Garnet is my choice for this recipe.
1 Tablespoon non-alcoholic Zinfandel wine
$1/2$ teaspoon onion powder
$1/4$ teaspoon gingerroot, peeled and grated
2 teaspoons tamari
$1/2$ teaspoon cumin
Pinch cinnamon
Sea salt to taste

Peel yams and cut into $1/2$" slices. Steam or boil until they're slightly soft, 12–15 minutes. Put all ingredients in blender and mix until of purée consistency.

See picture, page 87

Salads & Dressings

"The foods whose calcium is best utilized are those highest in calcium-phosphorus ratio: green leafy vegetables."

— FROM *DIET FOR A NEW AMERICA,* BY JOHN ROBBINS

Sara's Mexican Salad, see page 104

Salads

"The one way to get thin is to re-establish a purpose in life."
— CYRIL CONNOLLY

TIPS & SHORTCUTS

❖ Salads in the form of raw vegetables and greens are best eaten before the rest of the meal because they're high in enzymes necessary for good digestion, especially of proteins.

❖ A vegetable containing a seed is called a vegetable-fruit. Some of these are tomatoes, avocados, cucumbers, and bell peppers.

❖ Vegetable-fruits combine well with either vegetables or fruits, but never melons.

❖ It's best not to eat vegetables and fruits at the same meal, as they require different enzymes for digestion. Combining them will cause intestinal gas.

❖ Raw fruits should be eaten separately from other foods.

❖ Melons should be eaten alone, and watermelons should not be eaten with any other melon—just by itself.

❖ Because it takes only 20–30 minutes for fruit to be in and out of the stomach, wait that long after you've eaten raw fruit before you eat other foods.

❖ It's best to eat spinach raw. Spinach contains oxalic acid. In its raw state, oxalic acid is alive, replete with enzymes, and not only beneficial but also vital in keeping the body functioning properly. Once it's cooked, however, the oxalic acid becomes inorganic, or dead, and becomes both pernicious and destructive. It often results in creating oxalic acid crystals to form in the kidneys . . . also called kidney stones. For your health's sake, it's best not to eat cooked or canned spinach.

❖ Avoid eating iceberg lettuce, also called head lettuce. It has almost no nutritive value, and because it's so compact and known to contain unfriendly microorganisms, it's sprayed far more heavily than other lettuce.

❖ If you use only part of an avocado, store the pit with the unused portion of the avocado in the refrigerator and the flesh will not darken.

❖ How to ripen a rock-hard avocado: Put it in a brown paper bag, write the day's date on the bag, close it tightly, and put it in a dark place. I tuck mine in a corner of my herb cupboard. Peek at the avocados every day or two to see how ripe they are. Their ripening is hastened by the concentrated and confined gases they exhale.

❖ Refrigerate but do not ever freeze an avocado.

❖ Before adding dressing, sprinkle nutritional yeast over the salad and toss it well. It not only adds a subtle nut-like flavor, but it's a rich source of vitamin B12.

GREENS

Combine these freely for variety in flavor, texture, and appearance:

❖ Romaine lettuce
❖ Baby dandelion greens
❖ Baby beet greens
❖ Butter lettuce
❖ Red leaf lettuce
❖ Green leaf lettuce
❖ Watercress
❖ Escarole
❖ Raddichio
❖ Sprouts of all kinds
❖ Nasturtium leaves

SALAD TOPPINGS

Be creative!

❖ Croutons (recipes follow)
❖ Soy-based (TVP) bacon bits
❖ Pine nuts (pignolas)
❖ Crispy chow mein noodles
❖ Sunflower seeds
❖ Sesame seeds

SALAD TOPPINGS: CROUTONS

GARLIC CROUTONS

- **PREPARATION TIME: 5 minutes**
- **COOKING TIME: About 7 minutes**
- **YIELD: About 4 cups**

10 slices whole-wheat multi-seed bread, cut into 1" cubes.
2 Tablespoons extra virgin olive oil
3 cloves minced garlic, or 1/2 teaspoon garlic powder

Heat oil until hot but not smoking, then toss in garlic and bread cubes. Turn regularly for 5–7 minutes or until browned. Blot on brown bag or clean towel to absorb excess oil.

You may want to make lots more of these croutons than you think you will need, especially if you or your family like garlic. In the short time it takes to make them, the kitchen fills with a magnificent aroma—the kind that magnetizes garlic-loving nibblers! My kids used to call themselves "taste-testers," commenting, "I'm just checking to make sure you added enough garlic, Mom!" I started with three loaves of bread . . .

BAKED HERB CROUTONS

Whole, these go well on soups and salads. Crushed, they can be used as a filler in burgers, casseroles, lentil or nut loaves, and as a spunky topping over vegetables.

- **PREPARATION TIME: 10 minutes**
- **BAKING TIME: About 30 minutes**
- **YIELD: Four cups**

2 teaspoons garlic powder
2 teaspoons onion powder
1 teaspoon dried dill weed
1 Tablespoon ground thyme
1/2 teaspoon ground oregano
1 teaspoon dried basil
1 teaspoon paprika (Hungarian, if available)
10 slices whole-wheat bread (not sprouted)
1/4 cup **Ghee** (see pg. 40) or butter, softened at room
 temperature

Preheat oven to 325°. Combine herbs in a small brown bag and shake until they're well mixed. Spread a light layer of ghee on one side of each bread slice. Cut bread into 1" cubes and toss about a cupful at a time into the bag with the herbs. Shake it vigorously. Make the croutons a single layer on a non-aluminum baking sheet. Bake in slow oven for about an hour. If bread is not quite dried all the way through, turn off the oven, leaving croutons inside to finish drying out. You want them to be toasty. I store mine in pretty jars.

Caveat: Any bread that's to be made into oven-dried toast needs a relatively high gluten content to maintain its moisture. Because the gluten content is almost zero in sprouted breads, when dry-toasted they become as hard as stones. Bad for the teeth!

SALAD PREPARATION

One of the secrets to having your salad greens retain maximum flavor and crispness is to wash them as soon as you get them home. Another advantage of washing them right away and storing them is that they're ready at a moment's notice.

Fill your kitchen sink with cold water. Add one Tablespoon apple cider vinegar. This will kill parasites and does not affect the flavor of the lettuce. Cut away the bottom core of lettuce or similar green; remove root stems of spinach. Add these discards to your soup stock vegetable collection. Let the leaves soak a few minutes, then swish them around to remove any bugs or soil. Check that each leaf is clean when you remove it from the water. Rinse with clear water one last time.

Spin or blot greens dry. Place clean cloth in an airtight container, add greens, and store in the refrigerator until you're ready to use them. When you're ready to serve the greens, tear them—do not slice or chop. Not only is the salad more natural in appearance, but the leaves will not be bruised or discolored around the edges.

Sara's Thai Noodle Salad, see page 96

SARA'S THAI NOODLE SALAD

This salad created by my daughter Sara is the talk of any party, potluck gathering, or dinner. I have yet to meet anyone who didn't like it.

- **PREPARATION TIME: 15 minutes**
- **COOKING TIME: 10 minutes**
- **SERVES: 8–10**

THE SALAD

1 pound sesame noodles

1 large red bell pepper, diced

1 large green bell pepper, diced

2 ribs celery, chopped

1 bunch cilantro, chopped

2 cups whole roasted peanuts

1 large carrot, grated

One 8-ounce jar chopped pimientos

THE DRESSING

1/2 cup tamari

1/2 cup sesame oil

1/2 cup peanut butter

1/3 cup brown sugar

2 teaspoons crushed red pepper flakes

1 Tablespoon dry mustard

Cook noodles until done. Rinse in cold water and set aside. Prepare bell peppers, celery, cilantro, and carrots and put in large bowl. Stir in the noodles, peanuts, and pimientos. In a small bowl, mix the rest of the ingredients well, and add to the vegetable mix. Stir gently, enjoy, and let the compliments roll!

See picture, page 95

MARINATED AVOCADO & TOMATO SALAD

A natural picnic favorite. Marvelous on a hot summer afternoon served on a bed of wildly assorted greens.

- **PREPARATION TIME: 15 minutes**
- **CHILL: 1 hour**
- **SERVES: 6**

2 large, ripe avocados
6 medium tomatoes
Assorted greens (choose for color as well as flavor)

Core tomatoes and slice thin. Cut avocados in half and slice lengthwise. Discard pit. Arrange tomato and avocado slices in a shallow glass dish.

MARINADE
2 cloves garlic, crushed
1 teaspoon sea salt
1 teaspoon dry mustard
1 teaspoon horseradish
1/3 cup fresh basil, finely chopped
1/3 cup lemon juice
3/4 cup extra virgin olive oil

Combine marinade ingredients in a quart jar and shake well. Cover avocado and tomatoes completely with marinade. Refrigerate covered, about one hour. Drain, reserving marinade for dressing. Serve on a bed of assorted greens.

CHINESE PEANUT SALAD

This salad is quick & easy to make and will be requested again and again. It's filling and substantial enough to be the main course of your meal. Make lots. It will disappear!

- **PREPARATION TIME: 20 minutes**
- **SERVES: 6**

2 cups water
1 cup bean threads
1 cup peas, frozen or fresh
1 head romaine lettuce
1 can sliced water chestnuts
1 cup fresh Chinese (mung) bean sprouts
1/2 cup roasted peanuts, crushed

Boil the water, then turn off the heat. Place bean threads in the hot water, breaking them in pieces. Let sit for 10 minutes. Cook peas. If frozen, follow package directions. If fresh, steam for 10 minutes. Set aside to cool. Wash lettuce thoroughly and break into bite-size pieces. Spin or blot dry. Place in large salad bowl and add drained water chestnuts, bean sprouts, and peas. Drain bean threads, and toss them gently with the salad.

For the dressing, use **Thai Peanut Sauce** (see pg. 121). Add to salad, toss well, then top with crushed peanuts.

See picture on next page

CHINESE PEANUT SALAD

Caesar Salad

A vegetarian version of a traditional favorite. Ideal with any pasta-and-marinara dish. Awe-fully good. Although most often served as the salad at a main meal, it's my favorite breakfast.

- **PREPARATION TIME: 10 minutes**
- **SERVES: Enough for one salad**

2 sheets dried nori*
One head romaine lettuce, washed well and blotted
   dry, torn into bite-size pieces
2 cloves finely minced garlic
3 Tablespoons extra virgin olive oil
1 Tablespoon Angostura's (vegan) Worcestershire sauce
2 Tablespoons fresh lemon juice
1 teaspoon Dijon (or other prepared) mustard
1/4 teaspoon Spike®
1/4 teaspoon sea salt
1 cup garlic croutons
Freshly ground black pepper

Place greens in a salad bowl. Hold nori over hot burner (gas or electric) for a few seconds until it turns toasty green and curls up a bit. Crumble over greens.

Combine remaining ingredients (except pepper and croutons) in a small jar, cover, and shake vigorously. Pour over salad greens, tossing well. Top with garlic croutons and a few twists of black pepper.

*See page 42.

COLESLAW

Goes well with baked beans and tofu hot dogs (commercially available).

- **PREPARATION TIME: 10 minutes**
- **SERVES: 6**

4 cups cabbage, very thinly sliced
1 cup seedless raisins
1 cup diced (1/4" cubes) cucumber
1 1/2 teaspoons sea salt (or to taste)
1/2 teaspoon black pepper, coarsely ground
1 Tablespoon brown sugar
1/4 cup **Tofu Mayonnaise** (see pg. 122)
1 Tablespoon apple cider vinegar
1/2 cup raw sunflower seeds

    In a large salad bowl, combine cabbage, raisins, and cucumber. In a small bowl, mix the salt, sugar, mayonnaise, and vinegar, using a fork, then a rubber spatula, to blend well. Add to cabbage mixture, stirring it in evenly. Sprinkle with sunflower seeds.

AMANDA'S BEAN THREAD SALAD

Although my daughter Amanda included this recipe in her own cookbook (The Gaping Halls Guide to Happiness, *1990), she invited me to include it here. A beautiful salad with unusual flavor combinations, it's the ideal companion for steamed or baked winter squash.*

- **PREPARATION TIME: 10 minutes**
- **SOAK TIME: 10 minutes**
- **SERVES: 4**

1 package bean thread noodles
1/2 cup green cabbage, shredded
1 tomato, sliced
1 cucumber, peeled and cut into 1" cubes
1/2 cup peanuts, ground

    Soak bean threads in hot water for 10 minutes, keeping water warm. Combine remaining ingredients in a medium bowl. Drain bean threads and cut into 1" pieces. Add to mixture in bowl. Done!

SWEET & SOUR BEET SALAD

This is a real taste treat for beet lovers—and we know who we are!

- **PREPARATION TIME: 15 minutes**
- **CHILL: If you choose; excellent served warm**
- **SERVES: 4**

1/2 English cucumber
One 15-ounce can whole baby beets
1/2 Bermuda onion, grated (as you would a carrot)
1 teaspoon dried mustard
1/2 teaspoon sea salt
2 Tablespoons apple cider vinegar
1 Tablespoon brown sugar

Using a fork, draw the tines down the unpeeled cucumber, scoring it. Cut into 1/4" slices, then quarter them. Combine cucumbers, beets, and onions in a 2-quart bowl. Place remaining ingredients in a small jar. Shake well and pour over vegetables. Eat warm or chill 2 hours . . . if you can wait!

TOMATO SALAD

*Goes well with baked potatoes topped with avocado slices and sprinkled with coarsely ground black pepper. Fabulous with dishes made with **Nutso Pesto** (see pg. 49).*

- **PREPARATION TIME: 15 minutes**
- **CHILL: 30 minutes**
- **SERVES: 4**

6 large tomatoes, chopped
1 onion, minced
1 teaspoon sea salt
1 1/2 Tablespoons apple cider vinegar
6 Tablespoons extra virgin olive oil
1 teaspoon black pepper, coarsely ground
1/2 cup fresh parsley, chopped
1/4 cup wheat germ
1 bunch spinach

Toss all ingredients together except wheat germ and spinach. Sprinkle wheat germ over top and mix gently. Serve on a bed of fresh spinach leaves. Chill 30 minutes before serving.

ALOHA DELIGHT SALAD, SEE PAGE 105

Sara's Mexican Salad

Deliciosa tossed with **Basic French Dressing** *(see pg. 114). Although it's filling enough to be an entrée, teens-with-hollow-legs especially love it with* **Tofuchiladas** *(see pg. 58). Quick, easy, and absolutely delicious.*

- **PREPARATION TIME: 15 minutes**
- **SERVES: 6 teens or 8 adults**

$1/2$ head each, romaine and red lettuce
3 tomatoes, chopped
One 6-ounce can pitted black olives, sliced and drained
2 avocados, chopped ($1/2$" chunks)
One 8-ounce can kidney beans, drained
One 8-ounce can garbanzo beans, drained
$1/2$ bag corn chips, crushed
Corn scraped from 3 cobs
$1/2$ Bermuda onion, thinly sliced
$1/2$ cup firm tofu, frozen, thawed, crumbled (optional)

Wash the lettuce well and tear into bite-sized pieces. Spin or blot dry. Toss with remaining ingredients in a large salad bowl. Add dressing and serve with additional whole chips.

See picture, page 90

Picnic Macaroni Salad

With its unusual flavor combinations, this salad is ideal for picnics as well as a summer afternoon meal served on a bed of raw spinach or lettuce. It may end up being your favorite macaroni salad.

- **PREPARATION TIME: 20 minutes**
- **CHILL: 2 hours**
- **SERVES: 8**

1 pound salad macaroni
One 8-ounce can tomato sauce
$1^1/2$ cups celery, diced
1 cup sweet pickle relish
One 8-ounce can sliced black olives
1 Tablespoon chili powder
1 cup **Tofu Mayonnaise** (see pg. 122)
$1/2$ cup Bermuda onions, minced
Sea salt and freshly ground black pepper to taste

Cook macaroni according to package directions. Drain in colander and rinse well with cold water. Combine remaining ingredients in a large bowl, mixing well. Add cool macaroni and mix thoroughly. Chill for 2 hours before serving.

Aloha Delight Salad

This salad is a natural choice for a summer luncheon dish.

- **PREPARATION TIME: 15 minutes**
- **SERVES: 6**

1 orange
3 firm, ripe mangoes
3 bananas
1 small pineapple (or one 8-oz. can pineapple chunks)
1/4 cup unsweetened coconut, shredded
1/4 cup walnuts, chopped
1/2 cup date pieces
3 Tablespoons honey
1/3 cup lemon juice

Peel, section, and dice orange. Peel, pit, and slice mangoes. Peel bananas and slice into 1/4" rounds. Drain pineapple, saving the juice, if you're unable to find it fresh. Put all the fruit in a large bowl. Add coconut, walnuts, and date pieces. With a fork, whip honey, lemon juice, and 1/4 cup pineapple juice together in a bowl and drizzle over fruit.

If you're making this for children, make extra. They really love it. They're especially fond of biting into the date pieces—and when they do, they grin as though they'd grabbed the gold ring on the merry-go-round!

See picture, page 103

Dressings

"To make a good salad is to be a brilliant diplomat:
one must know exactly how much oil one must put with one's vinegar."
— OSCAR WILDE

TIPS & SHORTCUTS

Salad Oils

❖ With all the concern over fat content in the diet, people often assume that no cholesterol means no fat. Wrong. No cholesterol simply means "not an animal-based product." All vegetable oils could have the tag "No cholesterol," but some are harmful to your health because of their chemical composition.

❖ Look for unrefined and organic wherever possible.

❖ I use only three oils: sesame oil, toasted sesame oil, and extra virgin olive oil. *Never cottonseed; never canola.*

❖ Here is some information you may want to remember about the two most widely used (read inexpensive) oils used in food products today:

Cottonseed Oil

This oil has the highest content of pesticide residues of any other edible oil. It also contains gossypol, a substance that irritates the digestive tract and can cause water retention and shortness of breath. This oil is used in hundreds—if not thousands—of commercial products from baked goods to commercially marinated artichoke hearts. Ingested consistently, it's a potential killer. *Read the ingredients on your labels.* You may be shocked.

Canola Oil

As this book was going to press, there was still a lot of hype about canola oil, actually called rapeseed oil. The Canola Council of Canada (CCC) renamed it canola after "Canada Oil." It has been known for centuries as an oil to be avoided, since it contains erucic acid, which, when consistently used in the diet, even in small amounts, causes fatty degeneration of the heart, kidneys, adrenals, and thyroid. It can also create permanent scar tissue in the heart. (Udo Erasmus, *Fats & Oils*). Less than 5% erucic acid is permissible by FDA standards because it's so harmful. Not only that, it's registered with the EPA as a pesticide.

True, canola oil is high in Omega-3 fatty acids, believed by some to reduce the risks of heart disease by lowering both cholesterol and triglycerides. If consistently present in the diet, however, "they

[Omega-3 fatty acids] may worsen blood sugar control, raise LDL [bad blood cholesterol] levels, and contribute too many calories." (Melinda Downie Maryniuk, E.Ed., R.D., quoted in the Winter 1991 issue of *Countdown*, a periodical published by The Diabetes Research Foundation.)

I suspect that one of the reasons canola oil is used so frequently is that it's cheap. High-quality oils are more expensive.

I went into all this detail because many people ask me what I think about canola oil, and you may have questions, too. Because it seems to be in everything these days, I read all labels carefully in order to avoid it. I would never put it in my body intentionally.

In 1996 I asked a kinesiologist friend to test it on some of her patients. She found that it had a negative reaction on 100% of the patients she tested over a month's time. Not 50%, not 85%, but 100%.

If you want to see the research for yourself, find a computer, access the Internet, and go to any or all of these sites:

• www.all-organic-food.com/canola/htm
• www.dldewey.com/canola.htm
• www.epa.gov.pesticides/biopesticides/factsheets/fs011332t.htm

Olive Oil

Because it's unnecessary for olives to be heated in order to extract their oil, olive oil is the only vegetable oil that can honestly be called "cold pressed."

There are four grades of olive oil: Extra Virgin, Fine Virgin, Plain Virgin, and Pure. All grades except Extra Virgin come from a second pressing, and are treated to reduce the resultant bitterness. For best aroma, finest flavor, and least toxicity (no preservatives or additives) Extra Virgin is worth the higher cost.

Safflower Oil

Safflower oil is good for sautéeing because of its high smoking point (500°).

Sesame Oil

Sesame oil has a luscious nutty flavor, regular or toasted. It's excellent for stir-fry dishes and sautéeing in general. The toasted variety is richer in flavor because the seeds are toasted before extracting the oil. Buy organic unrefined when possible. Ingested or rubbed on the skin, sesame oil gives a boost to the immune system.

Grapeseed Oil

Although it's a new kid on the block in the United States, grapeseed oil—a by-product of wine production—has been a favorite of European chefs for hundreds of years. It's high in natural vitamin E and the essential fatty acids necessary for normal cell metabolism and maintenance. It lowers the LDL (bad cholesterol), and is one of the few natural foods knownto elevate HDL (good cholesterol). "Grapeseed oil is a natural agent which raises serum HDL levels." (*Journal of the American College of Cardioology*, 925–116. 1993.)

SALAD VINEGARS WITH VARIATIONS

The only vinegar I use is apple cider vinegar, as all other vinegars interfere with digestion. If you want your vinegar to make a clear and rousing statement—and a wonderful gift—you might want to experiment in creating one that does just that. The vinegars listed here make delightful homemade gifts that will thrill any cook. Select a pretty jar, fill it with your homemade vinegar, and finish it off with a ribbon or other attractive tie-on. Truly a gift to be remembered! Use any one of these to suit your taste, or create your own.

Onion Vinegar
1/3 cup minced small white boiling onions
2 cups apple cider vinegar

(TWO WEEKS LATER . . .)
3 tiny white boiling onions

Combine the minced onions and vinegar in a jar. I find that a wide-mouth canning jar works best, but any kind will do. Screw lid on firmly, and store in cupboard for about two weeks. Stick a small removable label on the jar with the two-weeks-later date to make it easy to remember when the vinegar is done. When the two weeks have elapsed, strain the vinegar, discarding the onions. Peel three tiny onions and put them in an attractive jar of your choice, then pour in the vinegar.

Garlic Vinegar
12 cloves garlic, peeled and finely minced
2 cups apple cider vinegar

(TWO WEEKS LATER . . .)
3 whole cloves garlic, peeled and sliced in half

Follow directions for Onion Vinegar, substituting garlic.

Tarragon Vinegar
3 large sprigs fresh tarragon
2 cups apple cider vinegar

Place tarragon in pint jar and pour vinegar over it. Screw lid on firmly and store for two weeks before using it or giving it away.

Basil Vinegar
5 generous sprigs fresh basil
2 cups apple cider vinegar

Strip leaves from stems, chop well, and place in pint jar. Pour vinegar over them. Screw lid firmly on jar and store for two weeks.

(TWO WEEKS LATER . . .)
1 or 2 whole sprigs fresh basil, including stem

Strain, discarding leaves, and place 1 or 2 many-leafed stems of basil in jar. Cover with the seasoned vinegar.

This particular vinegar combines with olive oil as an exquisitely delicate Italian salad dressing. Add a few twists of black pepper and a dash of sea salt.

Here is an extraordinary vinegar, one you must try at least once:

Raspberry Vinegar

Using a pint canning jar (or equivalent), fill to the top with well-rinsed fresh raspberries, pressing them down firmly. Pour in apple cider vinegar until jar is full. Put the lid on, and set jar on a windowsill or other warm, sunny place for a week to ten days. When the time is up, pour vinegar through a strainer and discard berries. You won't believe the sumptuous flavor until you try it. Everyone who tastes this asks for the recipe.

VIM'S HONEY & MUSTARD DRESSING

Goes well with virtually any green salad.
Extraordinary as a dip with raw tofu cubes.

- **PREPARATION TIME: 10 minutes**
- **YIELD: About 4 cups**

1/2 cup honey
1 teaspoon sea salt
1/4 cup apple cider vinegar
3 Tablespoons prepared mustard
3 Tablespoons onions, chopped
1/2 cup water
1 1/2 cups sesame oil (not toasted)

Place honey, salt, vinegar, mustard, onions, and water in blender. Mix well. While mixing, add sesame oil in a slow, steady stream. Most flavorful when chilled a while before using.

VINAIGRETTE DRESSING

Goes well with virtually any green salad.

- **PREPARATION TIME: 10 minutes**
- **YIELD: 1+ cup**

3/4 cup extra virgin olive oil
1/3 cup vinegar of your choice (from pg. 108)
2 Tablespoons parsley, minced
1/4 teaspoon garlic powder
1 teaspoon brown sugar
1 teaspoon tamari
1/2 teaspoon dry mustard
Dash cayenne pepper

Shake well in a small jar. For optimum flavor, chill 1 hour before serving.

ITALIAN DE MILANO DRESSING

Especially welcome at any dinner with Italian food.

- **PREPARATION TIME: 10 minutes**
- **CHILL: 1 hour**
- **YIELD: 1+ cup**

1/4 cup extra virgin olive oil
1/8 cup apple cider vinegar
1/8 cup lemon juice
1/4 teaspoon sea salt
1/8 teaspoon black pepper, freshly ground
1/4 teaspoon garlic powder
1/4 teaspoon dried oregano
1 teaspoon parsley, minced
1 cucumber, peeled and cut into 1/4" cubes
6 tiny white boiling onions, peeled and quartered

Combine in a pint jar and shake vigorously. Chill 1 hour before using.

ONION, RASPBERRY, AND BASIL VINEGARS SEE PAGES 108—109, A GREEN SALAD, AND CROUTONS

No-Oil Italian Dressing

Goes well with just about any greens-and-raw-vegetable salad. You would be hard-pressed to find many calories lurking here!

- **PREPARATION TIME: 10 minutes**
- **CHILL: 30 minutes**
- **YIELD: 3/4+ cup**

1/4 cup water
1/2 cup lemon juice
1 teaspoon sea salt
1/2 teaspoon dried oregano
1/2 teaspoon dried sweet basil
1/4 teaspoon garlic powder
1 teaspoon onion powder

Mix in blender. Chill 20 minutes before serving.

Super Quick Sweet & Sour Dressing

*This dressing is truly vibrant! A natural with **Amanda's Bean Thread Salad** (see pg. 101).*

- **PREPARATION TIME: 5–7 minutes**
- **YIELD: 2 1/2 cups**

1/2 cup tamari
1/4 cup water
2 Tablespoons sesame oil
One 8-ounce can crushed pineapple with juice
1 Tablespoon fresh gingerroot, peeled and grated
1 clove garlic, minced
1/4 teaspoon crushed red pepper flakes

Spin in blender about 10 seconds. Great at room temperature, but chill if you prefer. Shake before each use.

No-Oil Tahini Dressing

This versatile dressing is welcome just about everywhere. It's lovely with tofu of all kinds, hot or cold, and is unsurpassed as a dressing on any green salad. Modified (see below) it doubles as a sandwich spread, and is especially tasty on rice burgers.

- **PREPARATION TIME: 15 minutes**
- **YIELD: 4 cups**

1 cup water
1 cup tahini
$1/2$ cup tamari
$1/2$ cup apple cider vinegar
$1/2$ teaspoon garlic powder
$1/2$ teaspoon dill weed
$1/2$ cup barley malt syrup
$1/2$ cup raw sesame seeds
1 Tablespoon Spike®

Put all ingredients in blender and mix. Not necessary to chill before serving.

One evening I was in a hurry preparing this dressing—my attention was elsewhere, and my memory was neither active nor reliable. As a result, I put in $1/2$ cup water rather than the full cup. Voilà! A sandwich spread was born! This dressing-spread has an absolutely enchanting flavor. Magic at its best.

Super Quick Sesame Dressing

- **PREPARATION TIME: 3 minutes**
- **YIELD: $1/4$ cup**

$1/4$ cup tahini
2 teaspoons apple cider vinegar
$1/2$ teaspoon honey

Whip ingredients with a fork until blended. You're done!

BASIC FRENCH DRESSING

*Goes well with just about any raw vegetable salad.
I often use it as a topping on my baked potatoes.*

- **PREPARATION TIME: 10 minutes**
- **CHILL: 1 hour**
- **YIELD: 1 cup**

1/3 cup extra virgin olive oil
3 Tablespoons apple cider vinegar
1 Tablespoon catsup
1 teaspoon sea salt
1/8 teaspoon black pepper, coarsely ground
1/2 teaspoon dry mustard
1 teaspoon paprika
1/4 teaspoon garlic powder
1 Tablespoon pimientos, chopped
1/2 teaspoon honey
1 Tablespoon minced bell pepper

Combine in jar and shake vigorously. Chill 1 hour before serving.

GINGER & LEMON DRESSING

Can be used as a stunning marinade for frozen tofu that has been thawed. A delicate complement to a raw spinach salad. Delicious over hot or cold bean threads.

- **PREPARATION TIME: 10 minutes**
- **YIELD: About 3/4 cup**

1/4 cup extra virgin olive oil
3 Tablespoons lemon juice
3 Tablespoons water
1 Tablespoon gingerroot, finely grated
1 teaspoon lemon peel, finely grated
1 clove garlic, minced
Sea salt to taste
1 Tablespoon tamari

Spin in blender 20 seconds. Tastes excellent either chilled or at room temperature.

Gravies, Sauces
& Condiments

"England has forty-two religions and only two sauces."

— Voltaire

Gravies, Sauces & Condiments

TIPS & SHORTCUTS

All the recipes in this section are touches that can transform an otherwise ordinary meal into a delectable feast. Not only that, every recipe in this section is geared to spending almost no time in the kitchen.

You can easily create a quick sauce or gravy ahead of time and store it in the refrigerator until you need it. A savory sauce can dress up vegetables and grains—even salads—and create a tantalizing meal.

Look through these pages until you find a sauce that suits your taste; you can whip it up in no time. Or, choose a sauce you really like and design your meal around it. Above all—enjoy!

BASIC GRAVY WITH VARIATIONS

BASIC GRAVY: ROUX

- **PREPARATION TIME: 5 minutes**
- **COOKING TIME: 10 minutes**
- **YIELD: 2 cups**

1/4 cup whole-wheat flour
1 1/2 cups hot vegetable broth
2 Tablespoons tamari
2 Tablespoons nutritional yeast
Sea salt to taste
1/8 teaspoon black pepper, freshly ground

In a heavy skillet (cast iron if you have one) over a medium flame, brown the flour. Use a wooden spoon to stir constantly until the flour becomes a rich brown color. Very slowly add hot vegetable stock and tamari, stirring constantly to avoid lumps. Stir in nutritional yeast and add salt and pepper. This gravy can be dressed up, down, or sideways, fitting just about any recipe that calls for gravy.

VARIATIONS

MUSHROOM GRAVY
Add 2 cups sliced mushrooms, sautéed, 1/2 cup sliced onions, and a diced bell pepper.

CARROT GRAVY
Add 5 carrots that have been steamed and puréed in a blender, with a pinch of nutmeg and a few shakes of apple cider vinegar.

SQUASH GRAVY
Add 2 cups cooked yellow squash that have been mixed in a blender, with 1/4 teaspoon garlic powder.

DO IT YOUR WAY GRAVY
Create your own using your favorite herbs and vegetables!

JEAN-MARIE'S MEXICAN SALSA

This awesome salsa can go from mild to hot, depending on your taste. So easy! So quick! So good!

- **PREPARATION TIME: 10 minutes**
- **YIELD: 3 cups**

3 medium tomatoes, chopped in small pieces
One 15-ounce can tomato sauce
1/2 cup fresh cilantro, chopped in small pieces
2 Tablespoons Bermuda onions, minced
1/4 cup green bell pepper, chopped in small pieces
2 cloves fresh garlic, minced
Pinch cayenne
1/8 teaspoon crushed red pepper flakes
2 teaspoons apple cider vinegar

Mix everything in a bowl. Flavor is enhanced if you chill before serving.

See picture on next page

VARIATION

Add a cup of cooked and mashed pinto or black beans and 1/2 cup of cooked corn for a real taste treat.

Goes well with corn chips, black bean chips, jicama, or other vegetable dippers. This is a pleasantly mild salsa, and is marvelous with any dish that calls for Mexican salsa or picante. If you like yours with more bite, either gently increase the amount of red pepper flakes, or add a jalapeño pepper or two (including the seeds), finely minced. The snappier you like it, the more peppers you use.

My oldest daughter, Jean-Marie, created this recipe. She's not one to spend much time in the kitchen, but she loves good food, so her recipes take a minimum of preparation and cleanup (shades of her mother), and they taste fabulous. As the oldest of eight children, she learned a lot of shortcuts along the way!

You might want to make this salsa a quart at a time, because everyone loves it; it also provides a marvelous snack at a moment's notice, and it disappears quickly. This phrase, a common one in our home, sums it up: "Hey, Mom! I thought you just made some salsa. The jar's almost empty!"

Jean-Marie's Mexican Salsa

CHINESE SWEET & SOUR SAUCE

Goes well over rice, noodles, or grains. Excellent with stir-fry vegetables.

- **PREPARATION TIME: 8–10 minutes**
- **YIELD: About 2 cups**

One 20-ounce can pineapple chunks, including juice
2 Tablespoons arrowroot powder
1/2 cup catsup
3 Tablespoons turbinado or brown sugar
1/3 cup apple cider vinegar
1/2 cup water

Drain pineapple and set aside. Put arrowroot powder and pineapple juice in a lidded container and shake well. Blend all ingredients, including pineapple chunks, in saucepan and bring to a boil. Reduce heat and simmer, stirring constantly until thickened and opaque.

QUICK & EASY NO-COOK TERIYAKI SAUCE

Ready in the blink of an eye, stores well in the fridge, and tastes so very good.

- **PREPARATION TIME: 5 minutes**
- **YIELD: 1 cup**

1/2 cup tamari
1/4 cup water
1 teaspoon gingerroot, finely grated
2 cloves garlic, finely minced
3 Tablespoons turbinado or brown sugar

Put all ingredients in a lidded jar, shake well, and bring to the table!

POLYNESIAN TOFU SAUCE

Sumptuous with steamed green vegetables; elegant served over Chinese snow peas and bean sprouts.

- **PREPARATION TIME: 15 minutes**
- **YIELD: 3 cups**

1 pound firm or extra firm tofu, drained, blotted, crumbled

1/4 cup apple cider vinegar

1/4 cup catsup

2 Tablespoons sesame oil

1 1/2 Tablespoons tamari

1 Tablespoon crunchy peanut butter

1 teaspoon honey

1/2 teaspoon prepared mustard

1/2 teaspoon prepared horseradish

1/2 teaspoon gingerroot, peeled and grated

1 clove garlic, minced

2 pinches cayenne

2 pinches cinnamon

Spin in blender until smooth. Heat, chill, or serve at room temperature. What a flavor!

THAI PEANUT SAUCE

Goes well over steaming hot rice, quinoa, couscous, Udon noodles, tofu of all sorts, and vegetables. Marvelous over fresh, raw, or lightly steamed peas or asparagus. Chilled, serve it as a dressing on an Asian salad. This sauce transforms a simple meal into a savory delight. I keep a can of coconut milk in the pantry at all times just for this sauce. Quick & easy, this recipe is a combination of the culinary genius of my daughters, Sara and Amanda.

- **PREPARATION TIME: 8–10 minutes**
- **YIELD: 3 cups**

1 can coconut milk

1/4 cup tamari

2 Tablespoons peanut butter

1 teaspoon ground coriander

1/4 teaspoon garlic powder or granules

1 clove fresh garlic, minced

1 teaspoon onion powder

Combine ingredients in saucepan and warm over medium heat for 7–10 minutes until peanut butter melts. This sauce thickens only slightly.

AUM-CURRY-AUM

This recipe is medium hot. Increase or decrease any of the ingredients to suit your own personal taste.

- **PREPARATION TIME: 5 minutes**
- **YIELD: Scant 1/4 cup**

2 teaspoons turmeric
2 teaspoons cumin
2 teaspoons coriander
1 teaspoon nutmeg
1/2 teaspoon cinnamon
3/4 teaspoon cayenne pepper
1/4 teaspoon black pepper, freshly ground
1 teaspoon sea salt

Measure into jar, put on the lid, and shake well to blend. That's it!

⁓

I simply love the flavors and foods of India. I love to prepare them, I love to smell them, and I love to eat them. I used to call this Vimala's Curry-in-a-Hurry, until one day I made a jar of it for my Sanskrit teacher. Wanting to decorate the jar Hindu style for him, I printed **Curry** in the middle of the label and put the Sanskrit symbol for *Aum* (a.k.a. "om") on either side. When my teacher looked at it, he said, "Ah! Aum-Curry-Aum. I like that!" The name stuck.

TOFU MAYONNAISE

Use this everywhere you customarily use mayonnaise. Tasty, quick & easy.

- **PREPARATION TIME: 7 minutes**
- **YIELD: 1 cup**

One 10-ounce package firm or extra firm silken tofu, squeezed and blotted
1 1/2 Tablespoons apple cider vinegar (or 2 Tablespoons lemon juice)
2 Tablespoons sesame oil (regular, not toasted)
1/2 teaspoon sea salt, or to taste
Dash paprika
Pinch black pepper, coarsely ground

Spin all ingredients in blender for 10–15 seconds, or until smooth. Will store covered in refrigerator for about ten days to two weeks.

For a zingy variation, add 1/2 teaspoon fresh dill or a favorite herb of your choice.

Brown Baggin' It

"A great step toward independence is
a good-humored stomach."

— FROM *DE BEATA VITA (ON THE HAPPY LIFE)*, BY LUCIUS ANNAEUS SENECA

Sandwiches

TIPS & SHORTCUTS

Bread is ordinarily what a sandwich is put on and held together with. *Read your ingredients* to make sure the product name or appearance of the package is not deceiving you, and avoid enriched flour at all costs. Many years ago, I read a definition of "enriched" that has remained with me: Imagine that you give someone a five-dollar bill and ask them for change and they give you a quarter back. That's the value you receive from enriched flour. There is no nutritive value, merely starch and empty calories. Know also that if the label says "caramel coloring," it's really saying "white enriched flour with coloring." Whole-wheat flour that is whole wheat has its own rich brown color, without any additions or modifications.

BREADS

If you can find sprouted-grain breads in your market, by all means try them. Also look for organic breads. When you find a sprouted wheat (or rye, barley, or corn) bread made from organically grown products, you've unearthed a gold mine. When bread is made from sprouted grain rather than grain that has been ground into a flour, the chemical composition is dramatically different. When any grain is sprouted, it becomes a vegetable in its simplest form, and it's the easiest to digest.

Many of the sprouted-grain breads are oil-free, and some are even flour-free. The textures are light and rich, and the flavor is incredibly pleasant. Some come temptingly unsliced and make a delectable bread that you can slice as thick or thin as you want. Great for **French Toast** (see pg. 137).

The Resources at the back of the book features a list of bakeries whose products I've used again and again. Each one of them bakes sensuous, healthful breads and bread products. No matter where you live in the continental United States, your grocer can get them for you. Tell your grocer what you want, and ask him or her to order it.

When my daughter Siobhan moved from California to Florida in the early '90s, she asked her local Gainesville health-food store to order bread for her from the Alvarado Street Bakery, a Northern California company. The market had it within five days. The proprietor was thrilled because it not only brought in many new customers, but it also ended up being his best-selling bread.

WRAPPING IT UP

Package your sandwich consciously. Help conserve natural resources by using a sandwich-size hard plastic, lidded storage container rather than using plastic or wax sandwich bags. These containers are a one-time buy and are usable for years. I've had mine for over ten years, use them all the time, and they cost only a few dollars.

For a lunch tote, use a canvas or string bag or a thermal lunch box instead of a paper bag. These are available in styles from simple to ornate, with prices to match. Use the lunch carrier that suits your needs. You can even include a cold pack kept in the freezer the night before.

The recipes I've included here are a few favorites, but they are by no means the only sandwiches you can create.

Experiment! From the spread you put on the bread to the way you transform it into a sandwich, do something new. Avocados with olives? Try it! Guacamole as a sandwich spread? Marvelous! Shredded raw zucchini with dill pickles, tomatoes, and cucumber slices? You might love it! This chapter is intended only as a guideline. Combine the raw foods you enjoy, and put them between two slices of bread.

POSSIBILITIES

Spreads
- ❖ **Tofu Mayonnaise** (see pg. 122)
- ❖ Green herb mustard
- ❖ **Split Pea & Sunnyseed Spread** (see pg. 129)
- ❖ Tahini spread
- ❖ Pimiento spread
- ❖ Guacamole spread
- ❖ Lettuce of any kind
- ❖ **Roasted Red Bell Pepper Hummus** (see pg. 126)
- ❖ Raw spinach
- ❖ Alfalfa or other sprouts
- ❖ Escarole
- ❖ Endive
- ❖ Radicchio
- ❖ Dandelion greens

Condiments
- ❖ Sweet pickle relish
- ❖ Catsup
- ❖ Barbecue sauce
- ❖ Dill or sweet pickles

Filling Parts
- ❖ Tomatoes
- ❖ Grated raw summer squash
- ❖ Watercress
- ❖ Cucumbers
- ❖ Sunflower seeds
- ❖ Avocados
- ❖ Olives
- ❖ Carrots
- ❖ Tofu slices

Add your own favorites to each list. Be imaginative. Experiment! Then keep the list handy for lunchmaking time.

If you include fruit in your lunch, eat it at snacktime rather than with your sandwich; fruits digest best when eaten alone.

ROASTED RED BELL PEPPER HUMMUS

This spread lends an exotic flavor to any sandwich, especially when that sandwich is made with tomatoes, alfalfa sprouts, avocados, and parsley. It's often used as a dip or filler for appetizers and is a natural filling for a pita bread sandwich. Great with dippers of celery sticks, jicama, or virtually any other raw vegetable. Versatility plus!

- **PREPARATION TIME: 5 minutes**
  (15, if you roast your own bell peppers)
- **YIELD: 2³/4 cups**

1 can (about 2 cups) garbanzo beans (chickpeas)
1 teaspoon sea salt (or to taste)
2 cloves garlic, finely chopped
2 Tablespoons lemon juice, freshly squeezed
1/2 cup tahini
About 1/2 cup water (add last)
One 8-ounce jar roasted red bell peppers (for a real flavor
   difference, consider making your own!)

Drain beans and rinse well. Put beans and other ingredients except bell peppers in blender and mix until smooth. Add only enough water for the consistency you prefer. Hummus thickens slightly as it sits, so if you're not planning to use it right away, make it a little moister than usual.

For variety, add 2 Tablespoons dried dill weed or your own favorite herb.

Add an 8-ounce jar of roasted red bell peppers and mix well, or roast your own! Here's how I make mine:

ROAST YOUR OWN RED BELL PEPPERS

- **PREPARATION TIME: 5 minutes**
- **BROIL: About 12–15 minutes**
- **YIELD: As many peppers as you choose**

Slice peppers in half lengthwise, remove the seeds, and place cut-side-down on a stainless steel cookie sheet. Broil about 6–8" from the heating element, checking on them every few minutes. As soon as the skins are well blackened, remove peppers from the oven and immediately place them in a brown paper bag. Close it tightly. The peppers create their own little steam sauna that loosens the skin. Wait about 3–5 minutes, then remove pepper halves one at a time, slipping off the skin. Discard skin. Chop, slice, or dice peppers, then add to hummus—or any other favorite dish. Once you make your own roasted red bells, you may never buy the prepared ones again. It's so quick & easy!

See picture on next page

Roasted Bell Pepper Hummus

PIMIENTO SPREAD

Excellent as a sandwich spread; perfect for stuffing ribs of celery. It draws comments such as, "What is this! I've got to have your recipe!"

• **PREPARATION TIME: 10 minutes**
• **YIELD: 2¹/₂ cups**

¹/₂ cup walnuts
¹/₄ cup almonds
¹/₄ cup sunflower seeds
¹/₄ cup celery
2 Tablespoons **Tofu Mayonnaise** (see pg. 122)
Two 2¹/₂-ounce cans chopped black olives
One 4-ounce jar diced pimientos

Spin walnuts, almonds, sunflower seeds, celery, and mayonnaise in a blender until well mixed. Don't blend it long enough for the nuts to become creamy; leave a few crunchy spots to add an appealing texture. Once it's all mixed, stir in the diced pimientos and chopped olives. This makes for an unusual touch of flavor in a sandwich, especially one that includes avocados. It also stores well in the refrigerator.

AVOCADO SPREAD

This spread is especially tantalizing in a sandwich made with tomatoes, alfalfa sprouts, mixed greens, and cucumbers. Also doubles as a fabulous party dip.

• **PREPARATION TIME: 5 minutes**
• **YIELD: About 1 cup**

2 avocados
1 Tablespoon freshly squeezed lemon juice
1/2 teaspoon Spike®
1 Tablespoon cilantro, chopped very fine

Mash avocados with lemon juice and Spike®. Mix well. Stir in cilantro.

SPLIT PEA & SUNNYSEED SPREAD

Amazing flavors occur when this is used on sprouted barley or rye bread.

- **PREPARATION TIME: 5 minutes**
- **YIELD: 1½ cups**

1 cup cooked split peas
2 Tablespoons **Tofu Mayonnaise** (see pg. 122)
½ cup toasted sunflower seeds, mixed briefly in blender
2 Tablespoons whole toasted sunflower seeds
½ teaspoon tamari
Dash of Spike®

Combine in small bowl and blend well.

TAHINI SPREAD

*See the variation of **No-Oil Tahini Dressing** on page 113.*

SOUTH-OF-THE-BORDER SANDWICH

*A beautiful partner for **Zingy Gazpacho Soup** (see pg. 68).*

- **PREPARATION TIME: 10 minutes**
- **YIELD: 1 sandwich**

2 slices bread
Tofu Mayonnaise (see pg. 122)
4 lettuce leaves, red leaf or butter
Enough slices of 1/4" thick tofu to make one layer
  on a piece of bread
Sprinkle of tamari
Cucumber, enough thin slices to layer on one slice of bread
½ avocado
2 Tablespoons **salsa** (see pg. 118)
1 clove garlic, mashed
2 thin slices Bermuda onion (optional)

Spread mayonnaise evenly on both pieces of bread. Place lettuce on top, then cucumbers, then tofu. Sprinkle tamari lightly over tofu. In a small bowl, coarsely mash avocado with salsa and garlic. Mix well. Spread this mix on tofu slices and top with the onions. Cover with second piece of bread and cut in half. Olé!

AVO-REUBEN SANDWICH

*This sandwich is a meal in itself, but if you're really hungry, serve it with a bowl of steaming hot **Broccoli & Barley Soup** (see pg. 70).*

• **PREPARATION TIME: 10 minutes.**
  A little longer if you broil it.
• **YIELD: 1 sandwich**

2 slices bread (sprouted-rye or pumpernickel are exceptional with this sandwich)
Tofu Mayonnaise (see pg. 122)
Stone-ground mustard
4 to 5 leaves red or green leaf lettuce
4 tomato slices
1/2 avocado, sliced lengthwise
1/2 teaspoon Spike®
1/2 cup sauerkraut (more, if you'd like)
1/4 teaspoon dill seed (optional)
1 Tablespoon sunflower seeds

Place sauerkraut in a small strainer to drain the juice. Do not rinse. Spread mayonnaise on one slice of bread, and mustard on the other. Place leaves of lettuce on either half, and put tomato slices on top, then avocado slices. Sprinkle them with Spike®. If you add dill seeds, mix them in with the sauerkraut before you arrange it on top of the avocados. Top with a sprinkling of sunflower seeds.

At this point, you have two choices: Either put the second piece of bread on top of the sauerkraut and cut your sandwich in half, ready to eat, or place both halves under the broiler for a few minutes until they're heated through. Then put the second piece of bread on top. Hot or cold, this sandwich makes a phenomenally pleasant and filling lunch.

See picture, page 23

GO LIGHTLY: BREAKFAST

"When you eat, eat slowly and listen to your body.
Let your stomach tell you when to stop,
not your eyes or your tongue."
— FROM *BUDDHA'S LITTLE INSTRUCTION BOOK,* BY JACK KORNFIELD

Comments

Breakfast, ah breakfast. When my kids were growing up, it was a given that we would all sit down at the same table and eat together—not only dinner, but breakfast as well. We always blessed our food and expressed gratitude for the gifts of life, good health, good food, and friendship. It was a bonding time for us all, as vital as the air we breathed. We shared, we talked, we laughed. With a crew the size of ours, it was a family rule that we all had to raise our hands to speak. In this way, the littlest ones also got their turn to participate. Vivacious, curious, and even a little outrageous, we had a good time when we sat down at table together.

At dinner, everyone ate what was served (if they liked it), but at breakfast I took orders. I look back and shake my head. I have no idea how I did it, especially on school days. But I did: scrambled eggs, poached eggs (we ate eggs in the early days), granola, fruit, oatmeal, wheat flakes. You name it and I prepared it. Even if they weren't hungry, my kids ate! I insisted that a good, sound breakfast was vital to health and well-being. My response now to my attitude then is, "Ah, how we learn!" Breakfast is not really necessary unless one is hungry, and then, it's best to go lightly. These recipes are the result of that newfound knowledge.

BREAKFAST BEVERAGES

Try any one of the following drinks as a zesty energy picker-upper and meal-in-itself, first thing in the morning.

In a blender, spin until creamy and smooth . . .
8 ounces orange juice or 1 cup pineapple chunks with juice

. . . with any one of the following:
10 raw almonds
or 1 Tablespoon raw pecans
or 12 raw pistachios
or 1 Tablespoon peanut butter

I've listed these fruit-juice combinations because they're known as energy boosters, and most people are accustomed to having fruit rather than vegetables in the morning. If you're one of those who prefers raw vegetable juices to raw fruit juices in the morning, turn to page 149 for a list of Creative Juices from Vegetables. Magnificent!

For a chilly morning when you want a nutritional, great-tasting quick fix that's warm and substantial, you might want to try any of the hot cereals I've included.

Remember that the grain-and-dairy combination is one of the least-friendly-to-our-body-combinations we can create. Either eat your cereal just as it is with no additions, or use rice milk, soy milk, cultured soy (the non-dairy equivalent of yogurt), or apple juice.

For a scrumptious addition, add raisins, apple chunks, date pieces, or berries. You may be surprised that you taste the rich grain-fruit flavor rather than the milk-sugar disguise. If you really want milk, use soy milk or rice milk. If they're not available in your area, see the Resources section at the back of the book.

STEWED PRUNES

Prunes are not only for senior citizens! My kids and I really like these. We served them not only for breakfast, but also kept a bowl of them in the refrigerator as an after-school snack. Not only are prunes an excellent natural laxative, but they're loaded with iron. Loaded!

- **PREPARATION TIME: 3 minutes**
- **COOKING TIME: 30 minutes**
- **YIELD: 4 servings of 6 prunes each**

24 dried, unsulphured prunes
Boiling water to cover them
$1/2$ lemon, juiced

Put prunes in stainless steel or enamel saucepan, and add enough water to cover them. Bring water to boil, turn to simmer and cover. Let them simmer for 20 minutes. Add juice of $1/2$ lemon and let sit for another 10 minutes. They are delicious warm, and even better after refrigeration on the second day.

KILLER GRANOLA

As this granola bakes, the house fills with that unmis-takable "homemade" aroma. You are bound to hear a voice or two exclaim, "Someone's baking cookies!"

- **PREPARATION TIME: 10 minutes**
- **BAKE TIME: About 30–40 minutes**
- **YIELD: 2 quarts**

IN A 9" X 13" ENAMEL OR GLASS BAKING PAN, MIX:

4 cups rolled oats

1/2 cup unsweetened coconut, shredded

1/2 cup unsweetened wide flake coconut (optional)

1/2 cup raw hulled sesame seeds

1/2 cup raw sunflower seeds

1/2 cup wheat bran

1 cup walnuts, ground

2 Tablespoons cinnamon

IN A MEASURING CUP, COMBINE:

1/2 cup light sesame oil

1/2 cup honey

2 Tablespoons vanilla

AFTER BAKING, ADD:

1 cup raisins or date pieces

Preheat oven to 350°. Mix dry ingredients well. Pour wet ingredients over dry, mixing well with a large wooden spoon or rubber spatula. Make sure that the dry mix is coated thoroughly and evenly. Bake, stirring about every 15 minutes until the granola is the color and degree of toastiness you prefer. Once it's out of the oven and has cooled a bit, stir in one cup raisins or other dried fruit of your choice. Date pieces add a magical flavor.

⤲

This mix is great to carry with you when you're traveling and might be missing a meal. It's delicious, filling, and loaded with all the right vitamins and minerals, not to mention fiber and protein. A high-energy food, it's the mainstay of my diet when I go backpacking. It's a real energy picker-upper, and even a little bit is quite filling.

This granola is not the result of chance mixings; it took me four years to evolve to that morning when no one looked at their bowl of cereal and groaned, "What's that floating around?" This particular recipe was a unanimous winner.

When my daughter Amanda was assembling her cookbook in 1990, she asked for permission to print this recipe. She called it "Mom's Best-in-the-West Granola." The name that my daughter Sara and her twin brother Luke gave it was *Killer Granola*. In their teen jargon, there were few higher compliments. The name stuck.

See picture on next page

KILLER GRANOLA

Down-to-Earth Oatmeal

This recipe is for early-morning-hungry folks, and for boys who have turned 12 and seem to have a bottomless pit rather than an ordinary stomach. This combination was not only a breakfast favorite, but also a frequent after-school treat on cold days. Delicious and filling.

- **PREPARATION TIME: 15 minutes**
- **YIELD: 6 cups**

4 cups water
2 cups rolled oats, uncooked
$1/8$ teaspoon cloves
$1/8$ teaspoon allspice
$1/8$ teaspoon nutmeg
$1/2$ teaspoon cinnamon
$1/4$ cup raw sunflower or sesame seeds
1 teaspoon vanilla
1 apple, cored, unpeeled and diced
$1/2$ cup raisins

Boil water, spices, and oats together for a few seconds; then add seeds, vanilla, apple chunks, and raisins. Simmer for 3 minutes. Done! Needs no additions.

When my daughter Sara was about six years old, she went to a friend's house and was offered a dish of oatmeal for breakfast. The hostess asked if she'd like (white) sugar on it. Her response was to the point: "Oh, no, thank you. My mother uses only whole-wheat sugar."

FRENCH TOAST

An indescribable flavor combination that goes well with warm apple juice or cinnamon tea . . . and a group of hungry people! This is a fun breakfast for overnight guests.

- **PREPARATION TIME: 15 minutes**
- **BAKING TIME: 25 minutes**
- **YIELD: 6 thick slices**

6 pieces whole-grain bread, sliced thick
1/4 cup honey or barley malt syrup
1 cup fresh orange juice
1 teaspoon cinnamon
1/8 teaspoon sea salt
Ghee (see pg. 40) or butter to oil pan

Preheat oven to 400°. Mix honey (or barley malt syrup), orange juice, cinnamon, and salt in blender until smooth, and pour into a bowl. Dip thick slices of bread in mixture and let them soak for a few seconds on each side, absorbing the liquid. Place them on a non-aluminum baking pan that has been oiled with ghee or butter. Pour any remaining liquid over the bread before it goes into the oven. Bake for 25 minutes. Serve face down on a plate with homemade applesauce. Cheers will abound!

See picture, page 138

FRENCH TOAST, SEE PAGE 137

APPETIZERS

*"We should take just enough food and drink to restore
our vigor, but not enough to overwhelm it."*

— FROM *DE SENECTUTE (ON OLD AGE)*, BY MARCUS TULLIUS CICERO

Appetizers

TIPS & SHORTCUTS

Dips with mysterious flavors tend to be icebreakers at gatherings. "Have you tasted that green dip? I can't quite figure out the seasoning. Dill? No, not quite. What is it?" So many dips are simply variations on the heavy sour cream theme that those with an outstanding flavor become conversation pieces.

Another way to have your dips reflect their natural origin is to serve them in vegetable "bowls." I use red or green cabbage most frequently, but in the heat of summer, an oversized zucchini is also handy, as well as being an eye-catcher. Simply cut your vegetable of choice in half, scoop out just enough of the vegetable to create a bowl, and fill it up with dip. Save the scooped-out vegetable part to add to the dip or to your soup stock collection in the freezer (see pg. 66).

A small pumpkin cut in half is a conversation piece as an autumn dipping dish. Just cut in the same direction as when you cut off the top for a jack-o'-lantern, but farther down the pumpkin. For winter, several acorn squash in a bed of sprouts and greens are ideal. A banana squash lends an unusual shape, and the skin of a kabocha squash made into a "dish" looks like a fine piece of ceramic. Purple kale is dramatic any time of the year. Use your imagination and whatever suitable vegetable is handy. Have fun and be innovative!

TOFU SKINNY-DIP & VARIATIONS

This quick dip is exceedingly versatile and can double as a tasty instant topping for a variety of vegetables.

- **PREPARATION TIME: 5 minutes**
- **YIELD: About 1 cup**

BASIC SKINNY DIP
6 ounces firm or extra-firm tofu, drained and blotted
1^1/$_2$ Tablespoons lemon juice
^{1}/$_4$ teaspoon sea salt
Dash Spike®

Crumble tofu into blender. Add the rest of the ingredients and mix in a blender for about 20 seconds until smooth.

For some tantalizing varieties, start with the Basic Skinny Dip recipe and add ingredients to suit your taste buds.

VARIATIONS

ONION SKINNY DIP
Add ^{1}/$_4$ cup minced onion and a pinch of freshly ground black pepper.

GARLIC SKINNY DIP
Add 1 clove minced garlic and a few sprigs of fresh parsley.

GARLIC-DILL SKINNY DIP
Add 1 clove minced garlic, a few sprigs of fresh parsley, and 1 teaspoon fresh dill weed.

SESAME SKINNY DIP
Add 1 clove minced garlic, 1 Tablespoon tamari, 2 Tablespoons tahini, and 1 teaspoon toasted sesame seeds.

GINGER SKINNY DIP
Add 1 teaspoon freshly grated gingerroot, a pinch of garlic powder, and a dash of Tabasco sauce. This variation is especially tasty with long, lean slices of cucumber and jicama as dippers.

AVOCADO CUPS

Serve filled "cups" on a bed of alfalfa sprouts garnished with nasturtiums and calendulas, both of which have a snappy flavor and are totally edible. A salad of colorful mixed greens is the perfect accompaniment to create the perfect quick, light meal to serve on a warm day when you have friends over for lunch. Ideal, too, as the main dish when you hostess a luncheon. The blossoms not only enhance the appearance of the place setting, they also add a zesty flavor to the greens. Quick. Easy. Tasty. Beautiful!

- **PREPARATION TIME: 10 minutes**
- **SERVES: 6**

3 medium avocados
1/4" lemon slice
3 medium tomatoes, coarsely chopped
1 bunch scallions, chopped, including healthy green tops
2 Tablespoons fresh parsley, chopped
1 Tablespoon fresh basil leaves, chopped
Pinch dried rosemary, ground
1/3 cup **Italian de Milano Dressing** (see pg. 110)

Slice avocados in half lengthwise and remove pits. Be gentle as you scoop out the avocados into a medium-size bowl, as you will want to keep the shells intact; they're going to be your "boats." Mash avocados with a fork. Squeeze lemon over mixture. Add remaining ingredients, mixing well. Spoon into empty avocado half-shells. Serve as suggested above. This is not only a conversation piece; it will have your guests asking you for the recipe!

See picture on next page

Avocado Cups

SARA'S NOTORIOUS MEXICAN TOFU DIP

This dip created by my daughter Sara goes with just about everything: raw veggies, chips, or crackers. It doubles as a sandwich filling or as a spread over cornbread. A quick celery-stick-stuffer. Fabulous complement to alfalfa sprouts.

I often serve this dip in a scooped-out raw tomato on a bed of butter lettuce topped with sprouts and nasturtium leaves, with a few nasturtium flowers on the plate. It's both delicious and beautiful.

- **PREPARATION TIME: 10 minutes**
- **YIELD: 4 cups**

1 pound firm or extra-firm tofu drained, blotted, and crumbled
1 Tablespoon catsup
1 Tablespoon nutritional yeast
1 Tablespoon tamari
2 ribs celery, finely diced
1/2 cup salsa medium-hot (mild just won't do here)
1 or 2 Tablespoons **Tofu Mayonnaise** (see pg. 122)
   (Start with one Tablespoon; add another if you want to, after other ingredients are mixed in.)

Crumble the tofu into a mixing bowl so it's as smooth as possible without using a blender or food processor. Add remaining ingredients, mix it all together, and blend well. Now taste it using a chip as a dipper, and if you want more salsa, be sure to add it.

This dip has a distinct, almost addictive flavor. For people who are terrified of tofu, this dip is an enticing way of introducing them to it.

When Sara was nine years old, she ate a dip similar to this at a friend's house, then came home and began to mix it up herself, changing it here and there. We all loved it, and it soon became a family staple. I often served it as a main course with steamed vegetables and a green salad on the side. Even the most confirmed meat-and-potato eaters devoured it gustily, as long as we didn't tell them beforehand that it was tofu!

At that time, Sara was an avid Suzuki violin student. She wanted more than anything to participate in the annual week-long San Francisco Suzuki workshop, but as a single mother, I simply couldn't afford it. Around the dinner table one evening, we were pooling our ideas, creating the possibility for her to attend. A friend who had helped build our geodesic dome was eating with us that evening, and he casually suggested, "Sara, why don't you sell your tofu salad at the market?"

We all looked at one another, blinked a few times, and a business was born. Sara began selling her dip, which she called "Rodgers Mexican Tofu Salad," to local markets. Within five months, she had made enough money to finance her trip, including lodging, meals, and workshops.

SPICY BEAN DIP

She continued with the business and created what became a legendary product in the Nevada City-Grass Valley, California, area. You may still find "Rodgers Tofu Salad" in local health-food stores there, as she sold her business when she was 12. Although the new owners didn't change the name, through the years they did change the recipe. So, if you want the real thing—this is it!

This recipe launched Sara as "Tofu Queen" (as opposed to Burger King). Even today she can create tofu dishes unimaginable to even the most creative chef. All it takes is one person to say, "Oh, good—Sara's cooking!" and she's in the kitchen.

See picture, page 146

A natural with corn chips, bean chips, crackers, or jicama sticks as dippers. This dip is sooooooooo good.

- **PREPARATION TIME: 10 minutes**
- **COOKING TIME: 10 minutes**
- **YIELD: 6 cups**

4 cups cooked pinto beans, mashed
  (or one 32-ounce can vegetarian refried beans)
1 teaspoon sea salt
1/2 cup water
1 medium yellow onion, grated (as you would a carrot)
1 clove garlic, finely minced
1/2 teaspoon powdered cumin
2 jalapeño chili peppers, finely minced, including seeds
1 Tablespoon brown sugar
4 Roma tomatoes, chopped

Place all ingredients in saucepan; simmer for 10 minutes, stirring often. Remove from heat.

ADD:
Juice from one medium lemon
3 Tablespoons chili powder
1 teaspoon sea salt
1 Tablespoon sesame oil

Stir until smooth. Serve hot or cold.

Sara's Notorious Mexican Tofu Dip, see page 144

BEVERAGES

"The National Dairy Council would like you to think that without milk you'd soon become calcium-deficient and little more than a quaking mass of jellylike flesh, but the truth is almost the opposite. Where does a cow or an elephant get the calcium needed to grow its huge bones? From plants, of course. Only plants. Calcium deficiency of dietary origin is unknown in humans."

— FROM *THE MCDOUGALL PROGRAM*, BY JOHN A. MCDOUGALL, M.D.

Beverages

TIPS & SHORTCUTS

Vegetable Juices

Vegetable juices are delightful, refreshing, and exceedingly nutritious. They are the regenerators of the body. When fresh, raw, organic, unsprayed vegetables are used, they contain all the amino acids, minerals, salts, enzymes, and vitamins needed by the human body. More than that, they have intrinsic healing properties.

Used properly under the guidance of a licensed practitioner (chiropractor; kinesiologist; Ayurvedic, homeopathic, or naturopathic physician) who has personal experience with the healing properties of juices, you can be guided on a path to renewed health and vigor. If this appeals to you, I recommend Dr. Norman W. Walker's little book, *Raw Vegetable Juices* (Jove Publications, Inc. 1970, 1981). If it's out of print, haunt your local used bookstore until you find a copy. Dr. Walker, by the way, lived on raw vegetables and juices exclusively, grew his own vegetables, walked five miles a day, and was still writing books until he died in 1984 at the age of 118. I listen to people like that.

Fruit Juices

Fruit juices, like fruit, are blood cleansers. They're also sources of instant energy and vitality. The brain uses only one food: glucose. Fruit is glucose, so it's immediately available as a source of energy without having to be converted. Because fruit is predigested, it simply passes through the stomach, remaining there for about 20 to 30 minutes, on its way to the intestines. Once it reaches the intestines, it releases glucose into the body as energy. Non-fruit foods go into the stomach and begin the digestion process in order to be broken down for assimilation, a process that can take hours. Fruit juices are simply fruits in another form.

OTHER BEVERAGES

Water

Water of good quality is the finest beverage you can drink. With no additions, it provides the kidneys with a means to flush toxins from the body and keeps us from becoming dehydrated. *And* it contains no fats, no sugars, no caffeine, no phosphoric acid, and no calories. In order to lose weight, drinking water is a must. And to think—there are more substitutes for water than for anything else on the planet!

With drinking water as contaminated as it is these days, I strongly recommend bottled water or a home water purifier system. The system I use is a sink-top model and has a carbon filter that needs to be replaced every six months or so. It is well worth the investment. For detailed information on the quality of drinking water and available purifiers, go to your local bookstore, library, health-food center, or the Internet.

One last thing about water. In the words of Andrew Weil, M.D., in his book *Natural Health, Natural Medicine*: "Never draw water from the hot water tap for drinking or cooking, even if you are going to use it to make tea or boil pasta. . . . Water from the hot tap is unfit for human consumption, no matter what your pipes are made of."

Coffee, Decaf, Sodas, Phosphoric Acid

Caffeine and sugar are drugs; artificial sweeteners are poison. Phosphoric acid depletes magnesium and calcium and elevates blood pressure. There are countless sources of information available on all of this. If you want to read about their impact on your health, go to your local library and ask for books or magazine articles on the subject. They abound.

GET YOUR CREATIVE JUICES FLOWING

Vegetable Juices

Vegetable juices can be the most spectacular, delicious, and health-giving beverages imaginable. They're instantly vitalizing. Select the vegetables you enjoy, and create beverages you never dreamed were possible. Be sure to wash all vegetables very well, first with apple cider vinegar, then under cold running water, and (if they're not delicate like lettuce), scrub them with a vegetable brush. A natural fiber brush does an excellent job.

❖ Cut carrots about $1/2"$ below the collar, snip off the root tip, and use the parts you cut off for your soup broth vegetable scrap collection in the freezer.

❖ With beets, buy young ones, and use tops and beets in the juice.

Some Favorite Combinations:
❖ Carrot by itself
❖ Carrot, celery, and parsley (CCP)
❖ Carrot and celery
❖ Carrot, beet, and celery
❖ Carrot and beet
❖ Carrot, lettuce, and spinach
❖ Carrot and spinach
❖ Carrot, parsley, and spinach
❖ Carrot and parsley
❖ Carrot, spinach, and parsley
❖ Carrot and cucumber

Although I use carrots as the base of the juices I prepare, you can use whatever suits your taste buds. Experiment, and create them any way you prefer. Mix and match until you find a flavor combination you like, one that makes you feel good. For a long list of vegetable-juice combinations, open up Dr. Norman W. Walker's book *Raw Vegetable Juices*. Don't let the small size of the book fool you. It's the finest book I've found on raw vegetable juices.

For lots of Veggie Juice combinations, go to the Internet: **www.rawfoods.com** and click on "Recipes."

Fruit Juices

Although beverages are most agreeable to digestion when they are at room temperature, your body will not complain too loudly if you drink something cold now and again. Here's a fun idea that I've used for years, especially for holiday celebrations and gatherings in general.

Ice Cubes

When you make ice cubes, put a piece of fruit in each cube holder before you add the water: a strawberry or pineapple chunk for fruit-based punches, and a leaf of mint (spearmint, peppermint, wintergreen, orange mint, pineapple mint, or lemon mint) for herb-tea-based drinks. A wisp of lemon peel is a delicate touch for almost any tea.

The drinks I'm sharing here are meant only as guidelines; they're really an open invitation for you to create your own punches, teas, and beverages according to your taste. Invent fruit drinks for yourself and your family by making a list of your favorite fruits and berries, then begin combining them in juice form. I was helped in this regard by having children with expansive, limitless imaginations. If you're stuck for winning combinations, turn the kitchen over to your kids . . . and watch uninhibited invention take place!

CARROT JUICE, SEE PAGE 149

CRANBERRY PINEAPPLE JUICE

- **PREPARATION TIME: 10 minutes**
- **YIELD: Half-gallon plus**

1 cup frozen pineapple chunks
4 cups cranberry juice
4 cups pineapple juice

Spin pineapple chunks in blender and add to cranberry and pineapple juice. Mix and chill. Great party beverage.

To add magic: add small banana slices to your ice cubes.

GINGERY PEACHY PINEAPPLE JUICE

- **PREPARATION TIME: 10 minutes**
- **PRE-FREEZE peach slices**
- **YIELD: Half-gallon plus**

1 cup sliced and frozen fresh peaches
1 teaspoon peeled and finely grated gingerroot
4 cups unsweetened pineapple juice
4 cups orange juice

In a blender, spin peach slices and ginger. Add pineapple-orange juice to mixture and mix well. Chill.

Gourmet touch: Put tangerine segments in your ice cubes.

WATERMELON JUICE

"The true Southern watermelon is a boon apart,
and not to be mentioned with commoner things.
It is chief of this world's luxuries, king by the grace
of God over all the fruits of the earth. When one has
tasted it, he knows what the angels eat. It was not a
Southern watermelon that Eve took; we know it
because she repented."

— FROM *THE TRAGEDY OF PUDD'NHEAD WILSON,*
BY MARK TWAIN

This sensuous juice may just end up as one of your favorites!

DIRECTIONS:

Buy a watermelon. Cut it in half. Scoop out all the red pulp and begin feeding it into your juicer. Include seeds; they come out with the pulp and do not end up in the juice. Discard the rind. One medium-sized melon makes about a half-gallon of juice.

Innnnnnncredible flavor! If it sits a while, it will separate, so just shake it gently before you drink it. The flavor doesn't change a bit.

See picture, page 155

SMOOTHIES & VARIATIONS

We made smoothies in our family long before they had a name. They've been available in health-food restaurants for about 20 years now, but quite often they're combined with yogurt, which, when combined with fruit, can snaggle your digestion. For optimum taste and tummy-agreeability, be kind to your body and use fruit only.

Again, what I'm offering here are combinations that are intended only as guidelines. Use your imagination and combine your favorite fruits. Mix fruits that you may never have seen combined. Have a good time!

One important point to remember, however, is that melons should not be combined with anything else. Melons are intended to be eaten alone or only with other melons. Watermelon, in fact, is best eaten all by itself, not even in combination with other melons. People often tell me that they don't eat melons regularly because they get a stomachache whenever they do—especially from cantaloupe. I have never heard of this happening when melons are eaten by themselves on an empty stomach. Experiment and see what works for your body.

BASIC SMOOTHIES

Smoothies taste best when you use frozen fruit, but cold or room temperature fruit works okay, too. Try it both ways and you decide. Here are a few combinations that are tried and true:

IN A BLENDER, SPIN UNTIL SMOOTH:
12 ounces unfiltered apple juice
3 frozen strawberries
2 frozen banana slices, about 3" long

OR
12 ounces unfiltered apple juice
3 frozen banana slices, about 3" long
1 slice fresh pineapple

OR
12 ounces orange juice
3 frozen strawberries
2 frozen banana slices, about 3" long

OR
12 ounces grape juice
3 frozen strawberries

OR
12 ounces grape juice
3 apple slices, peeled, not frozen

Use your imagination . . . and your favorite fruit!

WATERMELON JUICE, SEE PAGE 153

MIRACLE GINGER TEA

This tea has an enticing flavor. It's lovely hot or cold, and is especially complementary to Asian dishes.

- **PREPARATION TIME: 5 minutes**
- **COOKING TIME: 7–10 minutes**
- **SERVES: 4**

4 cups water
1/2 cup Rice Dream beverage (soy milk will not work
  in this recipe)
1/4 cup honey
2" piece of fresh gingerroot, peeled and grated

Bring everything to a gentle boil, turn down heat, and simmer for 7–10 minutes. Strain before serving. Sip warm or cold.

The "miracle" of this tea is that it is a cure-all for flu-like symptoms, nausea, or an irritated stomach. Several years ago when a friend felt "flu-ish," I suggested that he prepare this tea then sip it throughout the day. To urge him on, I wrote a silly little poem just for him:

Miracle Tea, oh Miracle Tea!
A sip for you, a sip for me.
It cures the flu,
It heals the gout,
It turns your laughter inside out.
Before you know it,
Your body's well,
For Miracle Tea has cast its spell.

Miracle Tea, oh Miracle Tea!
A sip for you, a sip for me.
Ginger here and honey there,
A sensual mix that's oh so rare.
It lifts your spirits
and calms your tum
and makes your nose completely numb . . .
Miracle Tea, oh Miracle Tea,
I beg you, cast your spell on me!

I had no melody for this ditty until my daughter Amanda saw it, laughed out loud, and began singing it to the tune of "Oh Tannenbaum"!

CHAI GURU!

This is an excellent substitute for coffee, and helpful rather than harmful to the body.

- **PREPARATION TIME: 5 minutes**
- **COOKING TIME: 4 minutes**
- **YIELD: Serves 4**

3 cups water
4 whole cloves
1/8 teaspoon ground nutmeg
1/8 teaspoon ground cinnamon
1/8 teaspoon ground cardamom
1/2" fresh gingerroot, peeled and finely grated
1 Tablespoon (two tea bags) black tea
3 cups soy milk (rice milk is too thin for this recipe)
1 Tablespoon honey

Boil water with spices for 2 minutes. Add the tea and simmer for 2 minutes more. Add milk and heat until hot but not boiling. Add honey and serve. Oh, yum!

See picture, page 158

CHAI GURU!, SEE PAGE 157

Desserts & Breads

"A common bond that unites us all is a fondness for chocolate and the smell of baking bread."

— Vimala

Desserts

TIPS & SHORTCUTS

Over the years, I've discovered that when a meal is balanced and nutritious, the body doesn't look around for anything sweet. I used to bake cookies and cakes, cupcakes and pastries. But that was in the early days when I thought vegetarian meant only no meat. Although I don't fuss with sweets much anymore, I've included some very easy-to-prepare desserts that I bake for special occasions or at the request of my friends.

Raw fruit is often spoken of as an ideal light dessert, but it's really best eaten by itself. To have it after a meal can interfere with your digestion for hours. Eaten in combination with a full meal, it can cause incredible amounts of intestinal gas and digestive discomfort.

If you would like a healthful substitute for ice cream, there are two brands I've tried: One is made with rice and the other with tofu. When I told my kids this, they rolled their eyes and gave me that "Oh, no! Not again!" look. Honestly, you would never guess that these two frozen desserts are dairy-free. Each has a creamy texture and a wide variety of flavors. Try one of them just once and see for yourself. Just once. You'll never know if you don't take a taste!

The two products are *Tofutti* and *Rice Dream*. They have oodles of flavor choices, among them: Lemon, Chocolate Cookies, Vanilla Almond Bark (my favorite), Vanilla, Mocha Almond Fudge—and the list keeps expanding. See the Resources section for the addresses of these companies, and have your health-food store owner order their products for you.

HOLIDAY MINCE PIE

Although most people save it for the holiday season, I enjoy mince pie so much I eat it any time of the year. This recipe is fast, easy, and delicious.

- **PREPARATION TIME: 20 minutes**
- **BAKE TIME: 40 minutes**
- **YIELD: One 9" pie**

1 whole-wheat pie crust
4 medium apples, unpeeled, cored, and sliced
$1/2$ cup raisins
$1/3$ cup apple juice
1 orange, scrubbed, juiced, and grated
Juice from that orange
$3/4$ cup turbinado or brown sugar
$1/2$ teaspoon cinnamon
$1/2$ teaspoon cloves

Preheat oven to 400°. Put all ingredients in saucepan and simmer until apples begin to soften, stirring now and again, about 10–15 minutes. Pour hot filling into unbaked pie crust. Roll second crust flat, and cut into lattice strips about $1/2$" wide, as long as the diameter of the pie. Weave strips $11/2$" apart to create top crust of pie. Bake 40 minutes. If crust starts to burn, cover lightly with aluminum foil.

೨

Even as a kid, I loved mince pie. Just loved it. Once I became a vegetarian, I assumed I would never taste it again because it's laced with either suet or ground meat—sometimes both. I put it out of my mind. At some time in the early '80s, I found this recipe in a magazine, newspaper, or cookbook, and I was overjoyed! Although I've altered it slightly through the years, if I hadn't seen the original recipe, I wouldn't have dreamed that vegetarian mince pie was even possible. If it resembles your recipe, *Thank You.* I have used it hundreds of times and have shared the recipe as often.

See picture, page 166

Yam Pie

Although traditionally a holiday dessert, this was one of our family favorites all year round. Quick to prepare, its sumptuous flavor is enhanced when made with a graham cracker crust. Butternut squash may be substituted for yams.

- **PREPARATION TIME: 12 minutes**
- **BAKING TIME: 35–40 minutes**

One unbaked pie crust
2 cups cooked yams (the orange-fleshed "Red Garnet" are best for this recipe)
1 cup rice milk
1/2 cup brown sugar
1 teaspoon cinnamon
1 Tablespoon fresh gingerroot, finely grated
1/2 teaspoon nutmeg
1/2 teaspoon cloves or allspice
1/2 teaspoon sea salt
Egg substitute to equal 2 eggs (see **Blissful Brownies,** pg. 172)

Preheat oven to 375°. In a medium-size bowl, mash yams until they're no longer lumpy; add remaining ingredients (except pie shell) and blend well. Pour into unbaked pie shell. Cover edge of crust with foil to prevent burning; remove foil 10 minutes before pie is done. Bake until filling is almost set. As it cools, the filling will firm up. Excellent with **Sweet Whipped Tofu Topping** (see pg. 169).

Stovetop Baked Apples

Simple to prepare and delicious to eat, these also make a quick & easy breakfast.

- **PREPARATION TIME: 10 minutes**
- **STOVETOP-BAKING TIME: 20 minutes**
- **SERVES: 1 apple per person**

4–6 very large baking apples (Pippin or Granny Smith)
1 1/2 cups mincemeat or **Killer Granola** (see pg. 134)

Scrub and core apples, creating a hollow in the middle of the apple that will hold 1/4 cup filling. Stuff with mincemeat or granola. Place apples in a 10" lidded skillet or pan, and pour in 1" of water. Bring to boil, then reduce heat and simmer, covered, for 20 minutes. If you use granola and want a crispy top, once the apples are cooked, broil 6" from heat. Serve warm or cold.

See picture on next page

STOVETOP BAKED APPLES

Fruit

If you're a fruit lover but have never experienced the delicacy created by putting fresh frozen fruit through your juicer, this may thrill you. To my knowledge, the only juicer that can perform this transformation is the Champion. If you love fruit, it's well worth the investment.

When you freeze fresh fruit then put it through the juicer, the result looks like frozen yogurt, but it's really only pure fruit with no dairy products or additives. The taste? You be the judge. Personally, I enjoy the ohhhhhs, ahhhhhs, and delighted raised eyebrows from fruit lovers when they taste this simple creation for the very first time. "How did you do that?" "Do it again and let me watch this time," are phrases I've come to expect. It's truly unbelievable. Do it and see for yourself.

❖ Wash fruit
❖ For large fruit such as bananas or peaches, cut them into 3"-long strips about as thick as your finger
❖ For berries, leave whole
❖ Freeze until solid (overnight is best)
❖ Put through the Champion

Blend Your Favorites
❖ Bananas with blue (or straw-, or black-) berries
❖ Peaches with raspberries
❖ Peaches with plums
❖ Pineapple with bananas
❖ Your favorite berry with your favorite fruit

✑

For years, this is as far as my imagination took me. One evening a dear friend of the family, a monk, stopped by to visit as my son Mark was preparing to blend some frozen fruit. With a twinkle in his eye, Brother Prahlad casually inquired, "Have you ever tried peanut butter with those bananas?" Mark looked at the bananas, mentally pictured the peanut butter, broke into a huge grin, and a revolution began! Many of the combinations below are the gift of my-son-the-ingenious-flavor-blender.

As you feed frozen fruit pieces into the juicer, add any of the following items with your fruit, alone or in combination:

❖ Peanut butter
❖ Ground nutmeg
❖ Almond butter
❖ Ground cloves
❖ Cinnamon
❖ Grated gingerroot
❖ Vanilla
❖ Ground allspice

❖ Carob chips
❖ Shredded coconut
❖ Nut pieces
❖ Ground cardamom

One of my all-time favorites is frozen peaches with a few grates of fresh gingerroot and a little shredded coconut. Mix and match and create your own flavor magic!

Although I've included these frozen fruit creations in the Dessert section, for the sake of your digestion, they're best eaten as a between-meal snack item.

Holiday Mince Pie, see page 161

Basic Apple Crisp, see page 168

BASIC APPLE CRISP

An old-time favorite with a new twist.

- **PREPARATION TIME: 20 minutes**
- **BAKING TIME: 45 minutes**
- **YIELD: 6 servings**

TOPPING
1/4 cup **Ghee** (see pg. 40) or butter
1/2 cup honey
1 1/2 cups dry rolled oats
3 Tablespoons whole-wheat pastry flour
1 cup walnuts, chopped
2 teaspoons cinnamon

FILLING
10 large, tart apples (Granny Smiths or Pippins are best)
1/3 cup turbinado or brown sugar
2 Tablespoons lemon juice
2 1/2 teaspoons cinnamon
1/2 teaspoon nutmeg

Preheat oven to 350°. Melt ghee and honey together, then blend into dry ingredients. Set aside. Scrub apples well and core, but do not peel, them. Oil a 2-quart glass baking dish with ghee or butter. Slice apples thinly (1/4") and put them in the baking dish. Combine remaining ingredients in small bowl, mixing well, and distribute evenly over the apples. Bake about 45 minutes, or until the apples are tender. If topping starts to get dark too quickly, cover with casserole lid.

See picture, page 167

CRANBERRY CRISP

*I like to serve this around Halloween because it's so autumn-y. Goes well with **Sweet Whipped Tofu Topping**. This is also a potluck favorite.*

- **PREPARATION TIME: 20 minutes**
- **BAKING TIME: 30 minutes**
- **SERVES: 6**

6 large tart apples (Granny Smith or Pippin)
1 cup fresh cranberries
1 1/2 cups apple juice
2 cups granola
1/4 cup sesame oil (not toasted)
1/2 cup whole-wheat pastry flour
1 1/2 teaspoons cinnamon

Preheat oven to 350°. Scrub apples well, and core, but do not peel, them. Rinse and drain cranberries. Slice apples into 1/4" slices and place in bowl with cranberries. Mix them around with your hands, then pour into an oiled 9" x 13" glass or ceramic baking dish. Pour apple juice over apple/cranberry mixture. Combine remaining ingredients in a small bowl, mixing until blended. Sprinkle over apple/cranberry mixture and press lightly in place. Bake for 30 minutes.

SWEET WHIPPED TOFU TOPPING

This goes well with any foods you ordinarily would top with whipped cream.

- **PREPARATION TIME: 5 minutes**
- **YIELD: 2 cups**

1 pound firm silken tofu
2 Tablespoons lemon juice
1/4 cup safflower or sunflower oil
1/2 cup turbinado or brown sugar
1/4 teaspoon sea salt
1 Tablespoon vanilla

Crumble tofu into blender. Add remaining ingredients and spin till creamy. Chill well before serving.

Chocolate

Chocolate? Yes, chocolate. If you're an orthodox vegan, your eyebrows are no doubt raised. Well, just take a deep breath, read on, and let me tell you a little about chocolate before you consider passing by my recipe for brownies. This section is not meant to be coercive, simply educational—and a little bit of fun.

In the July 1997 issue of our local Mensa newsletter, I read an article by Robert Martinez, a member of the Maryland chapter. It was about chocolate. Paraphrased:

It appears that a chemical called anandamide is present in chocolate; its molecular structure is quite similar to the active substance found in marijuana. Not only that, medical researchers have discovered that all mammalian brains (including ours) produce anandamide. They also contain receptors that interact with anandamide to create a relaxing high, which prevents pain signals from reaching our consciousness. If this were lacking, even a simple cut would debilitate us with pain. He goes on . . .

In the April 15, 1997, issue of *Proceedings of the National Academy of Sciences* are the results of a study conducted by S. K. Dey and Patricia Schmidt of the University of Minnesota in Austin; it talks about their research with anandamide. They report that anandamide is localized not only in the brain, but that the lining of a woman's uterus produces it, also, in far greater quantities than the brain. The study indicates that fertilized eggs are drenched with anandamide while they're growing and developing.

As I began to read the article, I was amused; by the time I finished the last paragraph, I couldn't stop laughing. Why? Having studied Sanskrit and Eastern traditions for many years, it didn't take much pondering to know that this chemical produced by our brains in order to block pain signals, this chemical whose molecular structure resembles that of marijuana, this chemical with which we were all bathed in the womb, this chemical called anandamide found in chocolate— is derived from the Sanskrit word *ánanda*. Ánanda means "Divine bliss, utter and complete joy, absorption in the Divine Presence." It implies having transcended the material world and having entered into a peaceful state of Oneness with all.

Chocolate, anyone?

BLISSFUL BROWNIES, SEE PAGE 172

BLISSFUL BROWNIES

These brownies are more like cake than the chewy kind you may be used to. They are oh! so good.

- **PREPARATION TIME: 15 minutes**
- **BAKING TIME: 25–30 minutes**
- **YIELD: Sixteen 2" x 2" brownies**

4 ounces unsweetened chocolate
1/2 cup **Ghee** (see pg. 40) or butter
1 cup brown sugar
2 teaspoons vanilla
Equivalent of 4 eggs (use egg substitute, below)
2 cups whole-wheat pastry flour
2 teaspoons baking powder (non-aluminum)
1 cup walnuts, chopped (save some to sprinkle on top)

Preheat oven to 350°; put oven rack in the center of the oven. Melt chocolate and ghee together over low heat. Set aside for a few minutes to cool. Stir in sugar and vanilla, then egg substitute. Stir just until combined. Add flour, baking powder, and nuts, stirring only enough to mix well. Bake in an oiled and floured 8" x 8" non-aluminum baking dish until brownies test done with a toothpick. Despite the temptation to dig right in, let them cool for about 10 minutes or so before you cut them into bars. Ooooommmm . . . ánanda!

EGG SUBSTITUTE:
1/2 cup arrowroot powder
1/4 cup tapioca flour
1/4 cup slippery elm powder

Mix together well. Store in a glass jar in the refrigerator.

One Tablespoon of this mix plus 2 Tablespoons water equals one egg.

See picture, page 171

Breads

"When bread is in the baking, some parts of it split open, and these very fissures, though in a sense thwarting the bread-maker's design, have an appropriateness of their own."
— FROM *TO HIMSELF*, BY MARCUS AURELIUS ANTONINUS, A.D. 178

BREAD: THE EIGHTH WONDER OF THE WORLD

Here are a few breads that are fun and simple to make, especially if you're not familiar with bread-making. When I was in the thick of motherhood, I baked 16 loaves each Saturday. Looking back, even I don't know how I did it. Yet, in all the years I have turned out loaves, it continues to fill me with wonder that bread begins as an innocuous wet mass of ingredients, then, as they blend and interact, a new shape emerges. Have you ever watched yeast bread go through the rising process? It's a miracle in motion. As if that weren't enough, the smell of baking bread is enough to create peace in the world, for it touches that same friendly spot in us all.

CORNBREAD

Goes well with: soup, salad, Mexican dishes, or simply hot out of the oven as a tantalizing treat.

- **PREPARATION TIME: 10 minutes**
- **BAKING TIME: 35 minutes**

2 cups coarse cornmeal (polenta)
1 cup regular grind cornmeal
3 cups whole-wheat pastry flour
2 Tablespoons baking powder (non-aluminum)
2 teaspoons sea salt
3 Tablespoons turbinado or brown sugar
3 cups water
2/3 cup untoasted sesame oil (olive oil just won't do here)

Preheat oven to 350°. In a large bowl, combine cornmeals, flour, baking powder, salt, and sugar, mixing well. Pour liquid ingredients in a small bowl, mixing slightly. Add wet mix to dry mix, stirring very gently, only until lumps are gone. Oil a 9" x 13" glass baking dish and pour in cornbread mix. Bake 35 minutes.

QUICK & EASY SPELT BREAD

If your body is wheat-sensitive, this bread is the answer to your sandwich needs. It takes just a few minutes to mix, and tastes especially good when toasted. Many of the spelt breads I've found in local health-food stores are textured and heavy; this one is textured and light. Give it a go and find out for yourself! It takes only minutes to prepare. I first tasted this bread in my daughter Siobhan's kitchen; she was thrilled to share the recipe with me.

- **PREPARATION TIME: 8 minutes**
- **BAKE TIME: 50–55 minutes**

4 cups spelt flour

1 cup barley (or oat) flakes

1 teaspoon sea salt

2 teaspoons baking powder

1 teaspoon baking soda

1¼ cup soy milk, natural flavor

1 cup cultured soy (the equivalent of yogurt)

2 Tablespoons extra-virgin olive oil

Preheat oven to 350°. In a large mixing bowl, stir all the dry ingredients together. Add the wet ingredients and mix thoroughly just until well blended; do not over mix. Place in oiled 9" x 5" x 3" bread pan and bake. That's it!

The wheat we're familiar with is really a hybridized version of spelt. Spelt is the most ancient form of wheat, with its origins in Southeast Asia. It was brought to the Middle East more than 9,000 years ago, and has since spread all over Europe. The 12th-century healer, St. Hildegard Von Bingen, praised spelt as the grain most ideally suited for the human body. In America and Canada, until the last few years, spelt has been fed to racehorses and livestock as a replacement for oats. Once its nutritive and anti-allergenic properties became known, its popularity began to spread among humans!

KALEIDOSCOPE BREAD

A marvelous way to eat this bread is to toast a slice and top it with almond butter. It's also the ideal bread for sandwiches.

- **PREPARATION TIME: 20 minutes**
- **RISING TIME: 2 hours**
- **BAKING TIME: 45 minutes**

1²/₃ cups warm water (110°)
1 Tablespoon baker's yeast
1¹/₂ Tablespoons honey
1¹/₂ Tablespoons sesame oil
5 cups whole-wheat pastry flour
1 Tablespoon sea salt

VEGETABLES, FINELY MINCED:
2 medium Roma tomatoes
2 medium carrots
1–2 ribs celery
1 medium onion
¹/₄ green bell pepper
¹/₄ red bell pepper

DRIED HERBS:
2 teaspoons oregano
2 teaspoons garlic powder
2 teaspoons basil
1 teaspoon marjoram

Preheat oven to 350°. In large bowl, mix water, yeast, and honey and let sit a few minutes until foamy. Add all remaining ingredients, mixing very well. Once it's not too sticky, knead the dough on a lightly floured surface for about 10 minutes. When the dough becomes firm and elastic, roll into a ball and place in an oiled bowl, cover with a damp cloth, and let rise at about 85°. When it's double in size—about 90 minutes—gently shape into two loaves, and place the dough in oiled pans. Once again, cover with a damp cloth and let rise one more time. When doubled in size, bake for 45 minutes.

Bibliography

Corson, Ben et al. Council on Economic Priorities. *Shopping for a Better World.* Ballantine Books. New York, 1991.

Diamond, Harvey & Marilyn. *Fit for Life.* Warner Books, 1987, 1990, 1994, 1996.

Erasmus, Udo. *Fats & Oils.* Alive Books, Vancouver, 1989.

Ford, Robert S. *Stale Food vs. Fresh Food: The Cause and Cure of Choked Arteries and Related Problems.* Magnolia Laboratory. Mississippi, 1997.

Horsley, Gaye Deamer. *Commercial Foods Exposed: And How to Replace Them.* Hawkes Publishing, Inc. Salt Lake City, Utah, 1976.

Hurd, Frank J., D.C. and Rosalie Hurd, D.C. *Ten Talents.* College Press. Tennessee, 1968.

Kloss, Jethro. *Back to Eden.* Woodbridge Press. Santa Barbara, California, 1975, 1981.

Kornfield, Jack. *Buddha's Little Instruction Book.* Bantam Books. New York, 1994.

Lad, Vasant. *Ayurveda: The Science of Self-Healing.* The Lotus Press, 1985.

Lappe, Frances Moore. *Diet for a Small Planet.* Ballantine Books, 1971.

McDougall, John A., M.D. *McDougall's Medicine: A Challenging Second Opinion.* New Century Publishers, 1985.

———. *The McDougall's Program: Twelve Days to Dynamic Health.* NAL Books, 1990

Malkmus, George H. *Why Christians Get Sick.* Destiny Image Publishers, 1995.

Miller, Saul, M. D. and Dr. Jo Anne Miller. *Food for Thought: A New Look at Food and Behavior.* Prentice Hall, 1979.

Parrett, Owen S., M.D. *Diseases of Food Animals.* Review & Herald Publishing Association. Washington, D.C., 1974.

Pitchford, Paul. *Healing with Whole Foods.* North Atlantic Books. 1993. This is without a doubt *the finest and most thorough book on diet and eating habits.*

Pritikin, Nathaniel. *The Pritikin Program for Diet and Exercise.* Grosset & Dunlap, 1979.

Robbins, John. *Diet for a New America.* Stillpoint Publishing, 1987.

———. *The Food Revolution: How Your Diet Can Help Save Your Life and the World.* Conari Press. Berkeley, California, 2001.

Rodgers, Amanda. *The Gaping Halls Guide to Happiness.* Self-published. Palo Alto, California, 1990.

Rose, Jeanne. *Herbs and Things.* Grosset and Dunlap, 1972.

Science News, volume 153, No. 22, 30 May 1998. "Soy's Recipe for Health," pp. 348 ff.

Shurtleff, William, and Akiko Aoyagi. *The Book of Tofu.* Ballantine Books. New York, 1981.

United States Department of Agriculture. Handbook Number 456. "Nutritive Values of Portions in Common Units."

Walker, Dr. Norman W. *Raw Vegetable Juices.* Jove Publications, Inc. New York, 1970. 1981. May be out of print. It's well worth seeking it out in used bookstores.

Weil, Andrew, M.D. *Natural Health, Natural Medicine: A Comprehensive Manual for Wellness and Self-Care.* Houghton Mifflin Company. Boston, 1983.

Index

Products & Resources

Alvarado Street Bakery
500 Martin Ave., Rohnert Park, CA 94928
Large line of organic sprouted grain products:
Breads, bagels, tortillas, "Grinola," etc.

Arrowhead Mills
Hereford, TX 79045
High-quality organic products.

Beckmann's Old World Bakery
104 Bronson St., Santa Cruz, CA 95062
Best sourdough and rye combinations I've ever tasted. Indescribable! Really "Old World." Organic flours. Large selection of products. Old-timers.

Bragg Health Science
P.O. Box 7, Santa Barbara, CA 93102
Bragg produces apple cider vinegar, liquid amino acids, and organic olive oil. Superior products, a company of high integrity.

Rabbi Emmanuel H. Bronner
Box 28, Escondido, CA 92033
Products you can trust for purity. Dr. Bronner has been in business since 1949.

Carissa's, Inc.
P.O. Box 9065, Highland, IN 46322-9065
Luscious vegan cookies made with soybean oil (rather than canola oil) and other natural ingredients.

Champion Juices
Plastaket Mfg. Co., Inc. 6220 East Highway 12, Lodi, CA 95240

Earthsave
www.earthsave.org 1 800 362 3648
Founded by John Robbins in the mid-80s, Earthsave is one of the most reliable and best-informed sources on vegetarianism in the country.

Eden Foods, Inc.
701 Tecumseh Rd., Clinton, MI 49236
Top-quality variety of products. Old-timers.

Gayelord Hauser's Modern Products, Inc.
(Spike®), Milwaukee, WI 53209

Health Valley Foods, Inc.
Irwindale, CA 91706-7811
Health Valley products lean toward "bland." Their Amaranth Graham Crackers, however, are a little tastier than their other products.

Imagine Foods, Inc.
1245 San Carlos Ave., San Carlos, CA 94070
Rice Dream alternative to milk and ice cream. Good stuff.

Nature's Warehouse, Inc.
Sacramento, CA 95816
Fruit-sweetened cookies and snacks. Drawback? At publication date, they were still using canola oil in everything. *Check ingredients* to see if this has changed.

Quong Hop Tofu Company
161 Beacon St., South San Francisco, CA 94080-6921
They also put out soy products under the *Soy Deli* label. Products of highest integrity, I recommend them without reservation. They continue to use high oleic sunflower oil (which is very expensive) in their tofu burger products, even though canola is much cheaper. They keep their prices competitive and still maintain the highest quality. When I toured their factory, it felt as though I were tiptoeing back in history. I was greatly impressed with the people and awed by the tofu-making process.

Shiloh Farms, Inc.
P.O. Box 97, Sulphur Springs, AR 72768-0097
Exceptional line of bread products, many sprouted, using chemical-free, pure ingredients. A small Christian community, baking since 1942.

Tofutti Brands, Inc.
50 Jackson Dr., Cranford, NJ 07016
Awesomely good ice cream-like desserts.

Tree of Life
St. Augustine, FL 32085-0410
A growing number of foods, mostly organic. Excellent quality.

Westbrae Natural Foods
Carson, CA 90746
Top-quality products. Old-timers.

Things change. As this book was going to press, all the above information was valid. For your health's sake, keep reading those labels!

In Closing . . .

Thank you for inviting my family and me into your kitchen. My closing thoughts were expressed many years ago by a treasured mentor of mine—an emperor of Rome and a most noble soul:

Pass then through this tiny span of time
aligned with Nature,
and come to your journey's end
with a gentle grace,
just as an olive falls
when it is fully ripe,
praising the earth that nurtured it
and grateful to the tree that gave it growth.

— FROM *TO HIMSELF* BY MARCUS AURELIUS ANTONINUS, A.D. 178

Blessings and good health to you!

Vimala Rodgers

Other Hay House Titles of Related Interest

BOOKS

BodyChange™: *The 21-Day Fitness Program for Changing Your Body and Changing Your Life,* by Montel Williams and Wini Linguvic

The Body Knows: *How to Tune In to Your Body and Improve Your Health,* by Caroline Sutherland, Medical Intuitive

Eating in the Light: *Making the Switch to Vegetarianism on Your Spiritual Path,* by Doreen Virtue, Ph.D.

Heal Your Body A–Z, by Louise L. Hay

The Yo-Yo Diet Syndrome, by Doreen Virtue, Ph.D.

AUDIO PROGRAMS

Body Talk: *No-Nonsense, Common-Sense Solutions to Create Health and Healing,* by Mona Lisa Schulz, M.D., Ph.D., and Christiane Northrup, M.D.

Eating Wisdom, by Andrew Weil, M.D., with Michael Toms

Healing Your Appetite, Healing Your Life, by Doreen Virtue, Ph.D.

Live Long and Feel Good, by Andrew Weil, M.D.

Your Diet, Your Health, by Christiane Northrup, M.D.

<hr />

We hope you enjoyed this Hay House book.
If you would like to receive a free catalog featuring additional Hay House books
and products, or if you would like information about the Hay Foundation, please contact:

Hay House, Inc.
P.O. Box 5100
Carlsbad, CA 92018-5100

(800) 654-5126 or **(760) 431-7695**
(800) 650-5115 (fax) or **(760) 431-6948 (fax)**
Please visit the Hay House Website at: **www.hayhouse.com**